COUNTRY STU

KENYA

Heather Blades

Series Editor: John Hopkin

Heinemann

www.heinemann.co.uk/library
Visit our website to find out more information about **Heinemann Library** books.

To order:
☎ Phone 44 (0) 1865 888066
▤ Send a fax to 44 (0) 1865 314091
▢ Visit the Heinemann Bookshop at www.heinemann.co.uk/library to browse our
catalogue and order online.

First published in Great Britain by Heinemann
Library, Halley Court, Jordan Hill, Oxford OX2 8EJ,
a division of Reed Educational and Professional
Publishing Ltd. Heinemann is a registered
trademark of Reed Educational & Professional
Publishing Limited.

OXFORD MELBOURNE AUCKLAND
JOHANNESBURG BLANTYRE GABORONE
IBADAN PORTSMOUTH NH (USA) CHICAGO

Typeset and illustrated by Hardlines, Charlbury,
Oxford OX7 3PS
Originated by Ambassador Litho
Printed in Spain by Edelvives

ISBN 0 431 014213 (hardback)
05 04 03 02 01
10 9 8 7 6 5 4 3 2

ISBN 0 431 014221 (paperback)
06 05 04 03 02 01
10 9 8 7 6 5 4 3 2 1

British Library Cataloguing in Publication Data

Blades, Heather
    Kenya. – (Country studies)
    1. Kenya – Social conditions – 1963 – Juvenile
    literature
    2. Kenya – History – 1963 – Juvenile literature
    3. Kenya – Description and travel – Juvenile
    literature
    I. Title
    967.6'2'04

Acknowledgements
The publishers would like to thank the following
for permission to reproduce copyright material.

Maps and extracts
AA Publishing: **26** (*AA Pocket Guide*), **38** (*AA Guide*);
ActionAid: **27E**, **48B**; Camerapix Publishers
International: **24** (*Spectrum Guide*); The *Courier*
Country Report No.157: **44**, **50A**; Fair Trade: **35D**;
Financial Times 12/8/99: **56A**; Geographical
Association: **28B**; The Guardian 19/3/98: **15C**; The
Guardian 21/4/98: **4B**; The Guardian 23/10/99: **4D**;
The Guardian 27/10/97: **4A**; The Independent
13/5/96: **4C**; International Planned Parenthood
Foundation, *People and the Planet* (1997): **41D**; Kenya
Flower Council: **36A**; Langenscheidt Publishers: **24**
(*Insight Guide*); Observer Magazine 5/9/99: **26C**;
Oxfam: **48B**; Save the Children: **48B**; Tea Board of
Kenya: **34A**; WaterAid: **48B**; Worldaware/Care: **25C**,
54C; Worldaware/World Vision Group: **5F**

Kericho Estate Map (**34C**): Courtesy of Brooke
Bond Kenya Ltd

Photographs
Allsport/Darrell Ingham: **4C**; Camera Press: **7D**, **58B**;
Hutchison Picture Library/Crispin Hughes: **18B**, **23D**;
Hutchison Picture Library/Tony Souter: **7C**;
Hutchison Picture Library: **26D**, **46A (right)**; Images
of Africa Photobank/David Keith Jones: **17B**, **23C**,
33C; Images of Africa Photobank/Dominic Harcourt-
Wester: **36C**; Intermediate Technology/Simon L'epine
Ekless: **57B**; Panos Pictures/Alice Mason: **42A (left)**;
Panos Pictures/ Betty Press: **21C**, **42A (right)**; Panos
Pictures/Fred Hoogervorst: **14A**, **38A**; Panos/
Giacomo Pirozzi: **53A**; Panos Pictures/ Jeremy
Hartley: **6B (top and middle)**; Panos Pictures/Lana
Wong: **56A**; Panos Pictures/Liba Taylor: **44A (right)**;
Panos Pictures/Penny Tweedie: **46A (middle)**; Panos
Pictures/Peter Barker: **32A**, **44A (left)**; Panos
Pictures/Sean Sprague: **24B**, **52C**; Panos Pictures/
Trygve Bolstad: **34B**, **37C**, **39B**, **52A**; Robert Harding
Picture Library: **18C**, **26A**, **46A (left)**, **50B**; Still
Pictures/Adrian Arbib: **9C**, **12B**, **18D**, **33B**; Still
Pictures/Jorgen Schytte: **43C**; Still Pictures/ Kianne
Blell: **6B (bottom)**; Still Pictures/Mark Edwards: **26B**;
Still Pictures/William Campbell: **15D**; The
Geographical Association/Maureen Weldon: **29C**

Cover photographs:
Animals at waterhole – Corbis UK; Kenyan girl –
Panos Pictures/Crispin Hughes

Any words appearing in the text in bold, **like this**,
are explained in the Glossary.

Contents

1 INTRODUCING KENYA

Images of Kenya

▶ **What is Kenya like?**

▶ **What images do newspapers give us of Kenya?**

▶ **What images do people have of Kenya?**

People have different images of a country, depending on their experiences and contact with it. Most people in the UK only see Kenya through the images in travel brochures and TV programmes. Other people read books, newspapers, magazines or the Internet to inform themselves. Some people are lucky enough to have travelled to Kenya.

Several different images of Kenya, seen from different perspectives, are set out on these pages.

FLOOD HITS KENYA'S COASTAL TOURISM

First hit by political violence, now floods. Mombasa and Kenya's coastal belt has been declared a disaster zone by the Kenyan government. Torrential rains last week destroyed homes, roads and bridges, killing 25 people.

The Guardian, 27 October 1997

A

KENYA'S MARATHON MAN, COSMAS NDETI, STRIDES TOWARDS OLYMPICS

Long-distance runners to Kenya are what tulips are to Holland or kangaroos to Australia. It could be something in the blood or it could be something in the soil. But, whatever it is, they flourish in the heat and high altitude of their East African homeland.

The Independent, 13 May 1996

C

ROGUE ELEPHANT TRAMPLES KENYAN TOURISM HOPES

The hit-and-run tactics of an elephant are providing one more problem for Kenya's beleaguered tourism industry. Pushing through an electric fence and operating under cover of darkness, Nduiki (Boy) has destroyed crops, put two people in hospital and effectively imposed a curfew on local communities

The Guardian, 21 April 1998

B

CAMELS BRING BOOKS AND HOPE TO BARREN LAND

Mobile library offers way out to Kenyan students

It is lunchtime in Iftin primary school and scores of children race across the school yard towards the camels. The attraction is not the beasts themselves but the two large trunks of library books they carry. Four mornings a week the mobile camel library sets out from Garissa provincial library carrying hundreds of textbooks and story books for schools in the area.

The Guardian, 23 October 1999

D

'First Impressions', from a holidaymaker (Hannah, aged 15)

Arriving in Kenya, not really knowing what to expect, my first impressions were nothing like I had imagined. As I stepped out of the airport in Nairobi, the first thing that caught my eye was a big sign saying 'Beware of AIDS'. It terrified me, yet to the people living there, it was just part of everyday life. As we drove from the airport to our apartment, the reality about the way many Kenyans lived became so clear. On the edges of the roads houses were built out of any available materials. Little children ran around in rags with nothing on their feet. People were riding on camels and using donkeys to carry luggage. As we got out of the van we were travelling in we were stared at. I felt so spoilt with my expensive shoes and designer clothes. Yet none of it really seemed to make a difference – the local children were playing happily having a great time. It was just a different way of life.

E

Rose Obuyu-Meehan – a Kenyan living in the UK

Occasionally I get a yearning for the warmth and bustle of home. For roast meat, fresh lake fish, the smell of the earth after a rainstorm, my own language, my own culture. Sometimes I miss the constant chat and banter of my sister's crowded house in Nairobi or the spontaneity of a party back at home in the village. Most of all though, I miss the sun – being able to live outdoors most of the time and not having to endure the long, bitterly cold nights that you have here in the winter.

F

'First Impressions', from Robert (aged 16), another first-time experience of Kenya

What hit me first was the heat as we got off the plane at Mombasa airport. The airport was very impressive: it was built of marble, which made it cool and shady, and this was very welcoming. The security guards and airport staff were all in very smart uniforms, not really what I expected in a poorer country. Outside the airport things were very different. There were a few big banks in the centre of the city, like American banks, but the rest of the city looked more like what I would expect in a developing country. It wasn't until we were driving on the outskirts of the city towards our resort that we saw huge, very grand private houses. The hotels looked very luxurious. We stayed in a thatched villa which was in a small group around the best swimming pool I have ever seen. We could walk straight onto the beach and you could see the coral reef. There were roaring waves breaking out at sea and strange-looking small boats bobbing up and down. There were Kenyan children playing on the beach, they loved to come and talk with us and they spoke perfect English. They just wanted to talk about what our lives were like back in England. They were fascinated by aeroplanes and couldn't believe how big they were. The children were on their own, but they were not annoying or pushy. There were loads of security guards around the hotels and beaches.

G

FACT FILE

A mixture of cultures

Kenyan culture, particularly in the cities, has been strongly influenced by Western culture, which is a reminder of the colonial past. Theatre goers in central Nairobi are far more likely to see a play written by a North American or British author than one written by an African. Yet, in the Kenyan African communities there is also a vibrant tradition of community theatre where locally written plays are performed. The Travelling Theatre of the University of Nairobi promotes the oral culture of the Kenyan tribes. They have helped keep alive folk tales, myths, songs, poems, riddles and rituals. Kenyan children learn manners, customs and history through stories and songs recited in the evenings, usually at the home of a grandmother or older women in their community. Adults and children can all join in the story telling. The government has been keen to include traditional Kenyan culture alongside the popular Westernized material found in most Kenyan schools.

Traditional Kenyan music was introduced into schools and college curricula in 1988, and annual music festivals bring together many different forms of Kenyan music. Ngoma (drum and dance) music is the oldest tradition. Western pop is very popular with young Kenyans, in common many young cultures. However, Reggae, hip-hop, and ligala are also popular.

Links between Britain and Kenya

▶ How is Kenya linked to Britain?

Kenya is one of the 65 Commonwealth countries and a former British **colony**. People in East Africa have traded with other countries since ancient times. Portuguese sailors were the first Europeans to reach the region, in the fifteenth century. British explorers like Livingstone did not travel through East Africa until the middle of the nineteenth century. It was after this date that the East African countries, including Kenya, became colonies of the European powers (**A**).

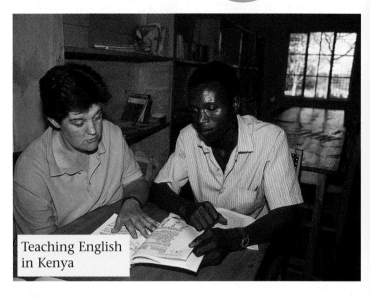
Teaching English in Kenya

In 1885 the Berlin Conference carved up Africa between Britain, France, Germany, Italy, Portugal and Belgium. A new frontier was drawn from the coast of East Africa to Lake Victoria, to the south of Mount Kilimanjaro, cutting through the Maasai grasslands. The area to the north of this line became the British colony of Kenya, and the area to the south became the German colony of Tanganyika (now Tanzania). In 1886 Queen Victoria gave Mount Kilimanjaro as a birthday present to her German cousin, so the border was redrawn. Many British families settled in Kenya in the early 1900s, attracted there by the fertile land in the region around Nairobi. The British government was keen to get British settlers in to Kenya.

In 1963 Kenya became an independent country, but it still maintains strong links with Britain (**B**). Many British families stayed on after independence, and still play an important role in the economy of modern Kenya.

A Historical information

A British volunteer optician at the Kikuyu Hospital in Nairobi

Expanding British rule
Kenya, along with many other African countries, was invaded by European countries in the mid-nineteenth century in the 'scramble' for Africa.

- By 1850 the Dutch, French and English had established trade routes leading from the coast deep into Africa's interior.

20% of Kenya's tourists come from Britain – the second highest group after Germany

B Some of the UK's links with Kenya

- Later in the nineteenth century, war began to rage between the local tribes, such as the Maasai, and the British. These wars disrupted the trade routes. The Maasai were no match for the British, and Kenya became a British protectorate in 1895.
- The British opened up Kenya for trade by building a railway in 1899 inland from Mombasa on the coast. Around 32 000 labourers from India were brought in to build the railway. The railway cost £5 million to build – it was funded by attracting British settlers to cultivate the land and grow crops for export. This was the first major 'white invasion'.
- By 1930 over 2 million hectares of the best Maasai and Kikuyu land had been taken over by the white settlers. The rich farming area in the Rift Valley had become known as 'White Highlands' or Happy Valley. Local tribes-people were removed or relocated into reserves where they were made to pay high taxes.
- Growing discontent led to a series of conflicts between the white settlers and the local people. One of the most important protest groups was the Mau Mau. During the Mau Mau uprising more than 13 000 tribes-people and 1000 settlers were killed.
- In 1952 the British banned all political parties, and anyone suspected of belonging to a party was imprisoned.
- By 1963 the British granted Kenya independence from British rule, and Jomo Kenyatta became the first president of the Kenyan National Party.
- When he died in 1978 he was succeeded by his vice-president Daniel Arap Moi.

C Colonial government building in Nairobi

D Independent Kenya – President Daniel Arap Moi with vice-president Mwai Kibaki

FACT FILE

Daniel Toroitich Arap Moi
Daniel Moi won his third term in office as president of Kenya in 1997. He was born in 1924 in Baringo district, north of the capital Nairobi in the Rift Valley. He was a schoolteacher before entering politics in 1955.

He was a member of KANU, the Kenya African National Union, when it was formed in 1960. It was this party which helped bring about Kenya's independence in 1963. Mr Moi became vice president in Jomo Kenyatta's government in 1967.

Amongst his achievements, President Moi introduced the idea of free education and free milk for all primary school children and doubled the number of primary schools.

2 THE PHYSICAL ENVIRONMENT

The landscape

▶ **What is Kenya's landscape like?**
▶ **How was the Rift Valley formed?**

Kenya is a country of dramatic landscapes. It covers a land area of nearly 600 000km² and contains a variety of landscape types (map **A**). The country has 20 mountain peaks over 2000 metres: the highest is Mount Kenya, at 5199 metres. This **extinct volcano** is the second highest mountain in Africa. To the north there are **semi-arid** plains and deserts, and the low coastal area is fringed with coral reefs.

The coral reefs help to protect the coast from the waves of the Indian Ocean. Coral reefs are living features formed by coral polyps which are sea creatures capable of secreting calcium carbonate to build an external skeleton. They only live in tropical seas between 30° north and 30° south of the Equator. Coral reefs are very attractive features, but they are vulnerable to damage from pollution and from the tourist industry.

Kenya has many other spectacular landscape features, including:
* the Great Rift Valley, which is so large it can be seen from the moon;
* Africa's largest lake, Lake Victoria, which has an area of 68 000km² – Kenya shares Lake Victoria with Uganda and Tanzania;

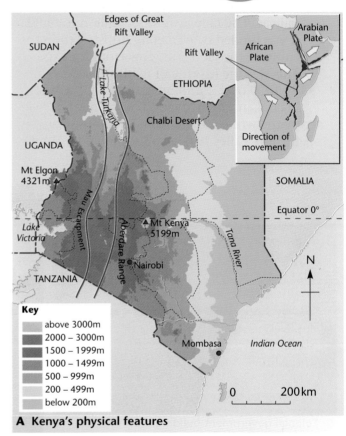

A Kenya's physical features

Key:
above 3000m
2000 – 3000m
1500 – 1999m
1000 – 1499m
500 – 999m
200 – 499m
below 200m

* Kenya's largest lake, Lake Turkana, which has an area of 8500km² and is famous for its wildlife;
* Kenya's longest river, the Tana, which has its source on Mount Kenya and its mouth in the Indian Ocean.

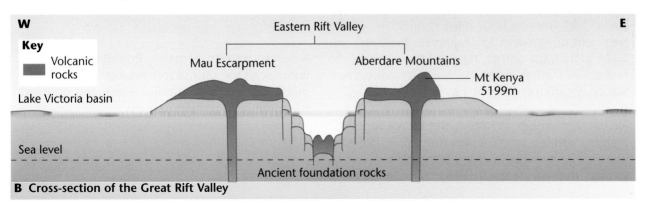

B Cross-section of the Great Rift Valley

The Great Rift Valley

Kenya is positioned near the edge of the African **crustal plate** (see inset, map **A**). The Earth's crust is split into 12 of these huge plates which 'float' on the underlying **molten magma**. The collision of these plates often causes the surface of the Earth to buckle into folds, and create a fracture or **fault**. This is how the Great Rift Valley (photo **C**) was formed. Around 70 million years ago the land in this area was fairly flat, but a series of collisions with neighbouring plates created a system of faults or cracks running across Africa from Ethiopia to Mozambique, a distance of some 3500km. Two of the largest faults were parallel to one another and the land in between them collapsed, forming the rift valley (figures **B** and **D**). The valley is between 60 and100km wide, with sides up to 3000 metres high in places. Standing on the edge of the Great Rift Valley is like standing on top of a cliff – these cliffs are called **escarpments**.

As the crust of the Earth was folded and faulted, magma from below the surface forced its way up through the cracks to form lines of volcanoes on the edge of the rift valley – this is how Mount Kenya was formed. Smaller cones were formed on the valley floor. Water draining into the rift valley became trapped and formed a series of lakes, including Lake Turkana.

C The Great Rift Valley

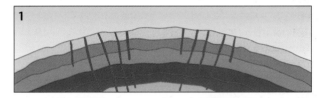

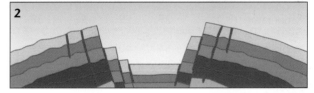

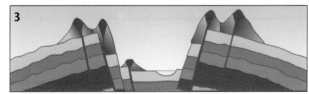

D How the Great Rift Valley was formed

FACT FILE

Mineral wealth in Kenya

The Kenyan government is encouraging private sector investment to develop mineral resources as a source of income and employment. A computerized database is being developed to give investors quick access to mineral information.

The most abundant and valuable minerals range from precious stones to industrial minerals:
- ruby – gem-grade rubies were discovered in Tsavo in 1973, but lower grades have recently been discovered in Kajiado and Kitui Districts;
- blue sapphire – first discovered in Kenya about 20 years ago, substantial quantities have been exported to Thailand. Recently their value has dropped, causing a major export problem;
- gold – found in alluvial deposits in rivers in a number of gold-producing areas in Western Kenya, where it is 'sifted' by hand;
- gypsum – a bulky raw material used in the cement industry. Mined mainly near Garissa and Malindi;
- lead – mined in the coastal region of Kenya, lead is used to make batteries.

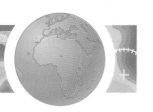

Climate

▶ What is Kenya's climate like?

"This is a country which has virtually no summer or winter; warm days happen all year round. As a rule you are sure of good weather at any time."
AA Guide to Kenya

The Equator runs through Kenya, yet most of the country is too high to have a typical equatorial climate. Most of the country has a tropical continental climate. The position of the overhead sun gives Kenya high temperatures all year round. The annual range of temperature in Kenya is much lower than the range in London (**A**).

Altitude plays a major role in Kenya's climate. Higher altitudes have higher rainfall and lower temperatures. The **lapse rate** – the rate at which temperatures decrease with altitude – is about 0.6°C per 100 metres. **Humidity** is also lower at greater altitude, which makes the higher lands around Nairobi a pleasant place to live.

	Jan	Feb	Mar	Apr	May	Jun	Jul	Aug	Sep	Oct	Nov	Dec
Nairobi (1661m)												
Precipitation (mm)	38	64	125	211	158	46	15	23	31	53	109	86
Temperature (°C)	19	19	19	19	18	16	16	16	18	19	18	18
Mombasa (sea level)												
Precipitation (mm)	25	18	64	196	320	119	89	66	63	86	97	61
Temperature (°C)	31	31	31	30	28	28	27	27	28	29	29	30
Kisumu (1135m)												
Precipitation (mm)	48	81	140	191	155	84	58	76	64	56	86	102
Temperature (°C)	29	29	28	28	27	27	27	27	28	29	29	29
London (5m)												
Precipitation (mm)	54	40	37	37	46	45	57	59	49	57	64	48
Temperature (°C)	4	5	7	9	12	16	18	17	15	11	8	5

A Rainfall and temperature figures for Nairobi, Mombasa, Kisumu and London

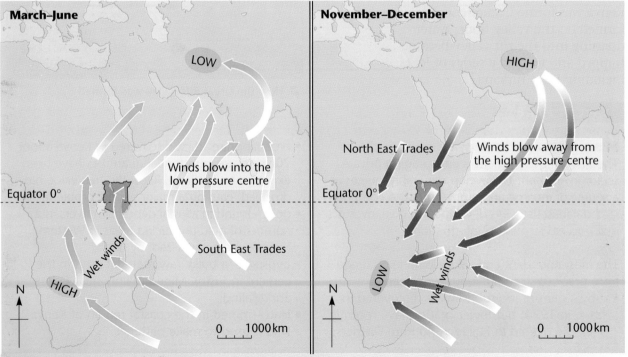

B Winds affecting Kenya's climate

The highest points, like Mount Kenya, have permanent ice and snow above 5000m. This level is called the snow line – the level above which snow and ice do not melt. As Mount Kenya is very close to the Equator, the snow line is at a much higher level than it is in the UK.

The effect of altitude on temperature is clear when looking at the the temperatures for Nairobi and Mombasa. Mombasa, only 16m above sea level, has higher temperatures than Nairobi, which is at 1675m.

The seasons in Kenya

The seasons in Kenya are not marked by a change in temperature as in the UK, but by a change in rainfall patterns. There are two separate rainy seasons caused by a change in direction of the **trade winds** (figure **B**):

- The longer rainy season from March to June is brought by the south-east trade winds. These rains are part of the Asian **monsoon** system. During June, when the sun is overhead at the Tropic of Cancer, the Asian continent heats up and a low pressure centre is formed by the rising warm air. As the south-east winds are dragged north into the low pressure centre,

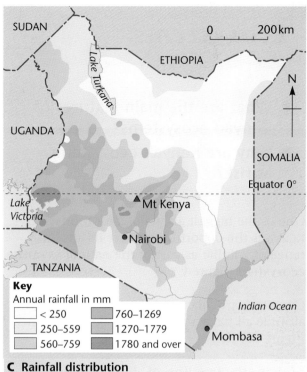

C Rainfall distribution

Key
Annual rainfall in mm
< 250, 250–559, 560–759, 760–1269, 1270–1779, 1780 and over

FACT FILE

Changing rainfall patterns in Kenya

The Department of Meteorological Change, based in Nairobi, tracked the changes in rainfall patterns over Kenya between March and May 2000, the period of the 'long rains'. In 2000 they arrived late, and in amounts well below normal levels in previous years. During May low rainfall was experienced over most of Equatorial East Africa. The rainfall totals for the season were below 75% of the average. Yet there were periods of heavy downfall in some coastal and western areas. These downpours, however, were so isolated that they have done little to improve the country's groundwater supply.

The lack of rain is thought to be connected with changes in sea-surface temperatures of the Indian and Atlantic Oceans caused by the La Niña event. La Niña is the opposite phase of the El Niño phenomenon, with warm temperatures in the equatorial Pacific replaced by cool, and the nature of the climate disruption elsewhere in the tropics and sub-tropics reversed.

they pass over the Indian Ocean, picking up moisture. These moist winds sweep in over East Africa as they move north towards Asia.

- The short rainy season in November to December is brought by the north-east trade winds. Now the sun is overhead at the Tropic of Capricorn. This brings a low pressure centre to the southern part of Africa and a high pressure centre over the colder Asian continent. The winds reverse, blowing from the high pressure to the low pressure centre. This brings drier winds, which pick up less moisture because they are cooler.

The **arid** north and north-east regions of Kenya have very little rainfall all year round (map **C**). Some areas, for example around Lake Turkana, have less than 250mm of rainfall a year: they are true deserts.

The social and economic impacts of rainfall shortages in Kenya may be devastating, increasing:
- conflicts over limited water resources and pasture
- crop failures
- power rationing
- the drift of migrants to the shanty areas of cities.

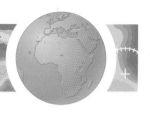

Ecosystems

▶ What are the main features of Kenyan ecosystems?

▶ Why are Kenya's ecosystems at risk?

One of the biggest attractions for tourists to Kenya is the opportunity to see its amazing range of wildlife as part of the natural **savanna ecosystem** (figure C).

Climate (particularly rainfall), soil types and altitude all have a major effect on ecosystems (figure **D**). Kenya's main ecosystems are:

- Above the **tree line**, at about 3000m, it is too cold for trees to grow, and open moorland ecosystems are common.
- In the highland areas above 1000m there are thick forests where the rainfall is well distributed throughout the year. The rainforests of the Aberdare Mountains west of Nairobi are home to abundant wildlife, including rare leopards. However, in some areas the natural forests have been cleared for agriculture and settlement.
- Along the coast, around Mombasa, thick **mangrove swamps** thrive in the hot, humid climate. These protect the shoreline against wave attack from the Indian Ocean.
- The desert and semi-desert areas of the north and north-east have a sparse vegetation cover. Most of the plants growing here have adapted to the arid conditions. They have long roots near the surface to tap all available water, and the leaf area is reduced to cut down water loss.
- The savanna grasslands are perhaps the best-known ecosystem in Kenya. This supports a range of large mammals that attract tourists on safari holidays. The rainy and dry seasons have their greatest impact on this ecosystem. The parched grasses die in the long dry season and then, as soon as the first rains fall, the grasses grow again. The hot, wet climate provides ideal growing conditions for grasses until the start of the dry season. The wildlife **migrate** seasonally with the rains.

Changing ecosystems

Changing climate due to global warming has been threatening ecosystems world wide, but perhaps the greatest threat to Kenya's ecosystems is from its people.

A Natural vegetation

SUDAN

Lake Turkana

ETHIOPIA

UGANDA

N

SOMALIA

Equator 0°

Lake Victoria

TANZANIA

Indian Ocean

0   200 km

Key
- Semi-desert
- Bush
- Savanna
- Mountain forest and grassland
- Desert
- Woodland/forest
- Mangrove
- Swamp

B Mangroves along the Kenyan coast

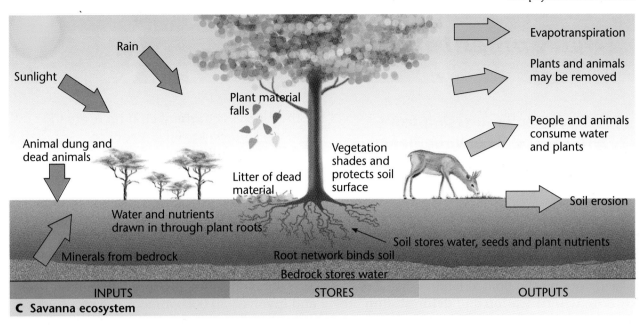

C Savanna ecosystem

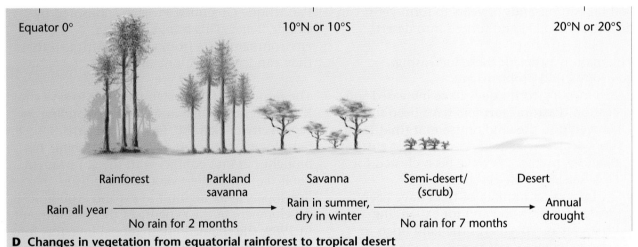

D Changes in vegetation from equatorial rainforest to tropical desert

FACT FILE

Mangrove swamps

Mangrove forest ecosystems line much of the coast of Kenya. Mangrove tree species are salt-tolerant, but are not true marine plants and thrive best around muddy estuaries where rivers bring in a supply of fresh water. They are a natural buffer to the erosive force of the waves from the Indian Ocean. The dense root network collects sediment and slowly advances the shoreline. They act as effective protection against storm and wave impacts on low-lying coasts. But they are also a refuge, a feeding ground and a nursery for many useful and unusual plants and animals.

Recently, however, many areas of mangrove forests have been felled to make way for tourist and industrial developments along the coast. The rate of felling has doubled since the mid-1980s, largely to build hotels and new housing. According to the United Nations Environment Programme, erosion now threatens some of the country's major resorts, which earn a large proportion of the country's foreign exchange. Geologists have written that the town of Membrui and much of the coastal areas to the south, including around Mombassa, could be swamped by coastal flooding as a direct consequence of removing the protective mangrove forests.

(Adapted from *People and the Planet*, vol 3, 1994.)

Environmental issues

▶ **Why is Kenya suffering from pressure on its environment?**

▶ **How can local projects combat environmental destruction?**

Around 80% of Kenya's land is arid or semi-arid and unsuitable for agriculture. With a rapidly growing population, increasing pressure is being put on the limited land available. **Soil erosion**, **desertification** and **deforestation** are growing environmental problems in Kenya. Soil takes thousands of years to form yet it can be quickly eroded and turned into desert.

The main reasons for these increasing environmental problems are:

• Bad farming techniques have increased soil erosion. **Pastoral farmers** have been forced to overgraze the land or use **marginal land**. Slopes have been cultivated without cutting **terraces**, and forests have been cleared for large tea and coffee estates.

• An increasing number of trees have been cleared for firewood and for expanding urban areas. This leaves the land open to erosion by wind and rain.

• A change in the global climate is causing more droughts than normal. This damages the ecosystems and soils in many areas.

• An increasing number of tourists are driven in trucks around the national parks. This damages the fragile vegetation. Tourism also means that wild animals are protected, and

they increase in number. If there are too many animals for the amount of vegetation, they strip vegetation and expose the soil.

Saving forests

Kenya's Green Belt Movement was set up by Wangari Maathai in 1977. Its aims are to save forests, replant forests that have been destroyed, and develop **sustainable** firewood resources. The Green Belt movement has set up over 3000 nurseries, produced 20 million trees and involved 50 000 women. The movement is now spreading across the continent via the PanAfrique Greenbelt Project, sponsored by Comic Relief. This brings together environmentalists from all over Africa so that they can learn from one another.

The most recent campaign has been to save the Karura Forest, 'a vital lung in the expanding capital city of Nairobi'. Professor Maathai's fight to save the forest from 'landgrabbing' has brought her into conflict with the government. Public land had been allocated to private developers in an attempt to expand economic development at the expense of the environment. In 1989, she shamed international investors into pulling out from building a 60-storey office block on Uhuru Park, the only green area in Nairobi's city centre.

A An area suffering from desertification/deforestation

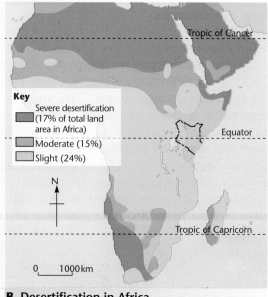

Key

- Severe desertification (17% of total land area in Africa)
- Moderate (15%)
- Slight (24%)

Tropic of Cancer

Equator

Tropic of Capricorn

N

0   1000 km

B Desertification in Africa

Saving the land
Terraces against time

Jane Ngei, a 30-year-old Kenyan mother and farmer, built her own dam with an ox-plough, spade and wheelbarrow. It's not a big dam; less than 15 metres across.

'It collects water running down the road after it rains,' she explains. It irrigates her half-dozen hectares of maize, vegetables and fruit trees, and keeps her small herd of goats and cattle watered.

Ngei's farm is one of hundreds located in the drought-prone hills of Machakos district east of Nairobi.

You might think this landscape would have turned to dust and blown away long ago. But these hills have not turned into desert. Today they are greener and more heavily planted with trees, more productive and less eroded than ever.

What went right? Some say that rising population forced farmers to change from cattle herding to settled farming. And it gave them the labour to work the land properly. The farmers have dug dams, planted trees and constructed terraces up the steep hillsides to trap rainfall and prevent the soil from washing away.

The Guardian, 19 March 1998

C Saving the land

D Women planting trees

FACT FILE

Sustainable soil conservation

By definition, sustainable soil conservation must involve local people, using local resources to promote present day use of the soil without risking its long-term productivity for future generations.

(SIDA) Swedish International Development Authority has been working in Kenya to promote sustainable soil conservation since 1974. By the mid-1990s over 30% of Kenyan smallholder farms had adopted some form of soil conservation. SIDA has worked with the Kenyan government and local farmers using local skills and resources rather than relying on imported technology and heavy investment from MEDCs. The 'Catchment Approach' is one of SIDA's most successful schemes. It involves identifying a river catchment area and working with the farmers in that area to develop sustainable soil conservation methods.

The catchment approach

A catchment area is identified and mapped out, ie. number and size of farms, slopes etc noted.

↓

Problems identified by the district agricultural staff, local administration and farmers' catchment committee.

↓

The local technical assistant collects detailed data from each farm.

↓

Intensive publicity to explain importance of soil conservation to local farmers carried out through ...

↓

A chief's baraza (a public meeting) – men attend the baraza as they are most likely to be owners but women do most of the agricultural work. Technical staff also visit farms to ensure message has got across. ⟷ Visit to a 'model farm' – Technical staff choose a 'model farm' in area to demonstrate different soil conservation techniques. ⟷ Field day tours – visits arranged to farms in other areas where conservation is already underway.

↓

Technical staff assist farmers to plan farm layouts, dig drains, terraces, choose trees and crops to plants.

↓

Structural work such as digging drains, making terraces often carried out communally, particularly by women's groups. Tools can be borrowed by District Agricultural Officer.

The North Eastern province

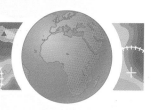

▶ How different is the North Eastern province from other parts of Kenya?
▶ What are the environmental problems in this area?

The North Eastern province is one of the largest in Kenya, with an area of 126 902km^2, yet it has the smallest population (554 000), and a population density of only 4 people per km^2. Conditions are harsh in this region, and it has the poorest provision of health care in the whole of Kenya (see map **C** on page 54).

Kenya is divided into eight provinces. Most of the North Eastern province lies in the semi-arid zone (see map **C** on page 11). Rain falls for only five months, with an average annual rainfall of less than 250mm. Temperatures are above 25°C all year round. This climate supports a bush-scrub type of vegetation. Farming is very difficult, but it is the main occupation of local people.

There is only one significant town in the area – Wajir – which lies towards the north of the province, on the main road to Ethiopia. Like most other urban centres in Kenya, Wajir has grown rapidly in recent years. In 1979 it had a population of 6834 which had increased to over 19 500 by 1995.

One reason for Wajir's rapid rate of growth is the changing lifestyle of the **nomadic pastoralists** in the area. The Rendille, Gabra, Samburu and Boran people have practised the same lifestyle for centuries. They have adapted to suit the harsh and fragile environments in the north-east by regularly moving their herds of camels to fresh grazing pastures. However, climate change, population growth and some well-intentioned aid projects (see below) have put the environment and traditional lifestyle at risk, so many local people are moving to the towns in the region.

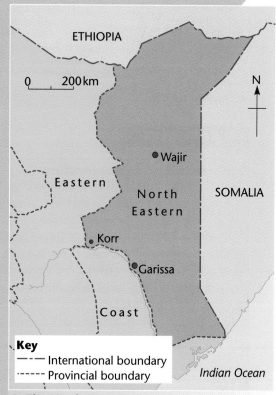

Key
—·— International boundary
------ Provincial boundary

A The North Eastern province

The Korr well project

Korr is a small village in the North Eastern province where an aid project went wrong. During the 1970s, new wells and a borehole were sunk in the village to provide a more reliable source of water. Instead of having to look for new grazing areas and water supplies as the rains failed, the local people now had a reliable supply. Nomads began to adopt a more settled lifestyle, and camels were sold in favour of sheep, goats and cattle. New settlers were attracted to the village by the promise of water. Shops and services developed in the village. Many of the traditional skills of the nomadic pastoralists were forgotten and not passed on to the younger generation.

However, a major problem was to find enough grazing land for all the livestock based in the village. Unlike the camels, the sheep and goats had to be brought back to the wells every couple of days. The area closest to the village was most favoured, so it was soon overgrazed. With increasing drought, soil erosion became a major problem. Soon an area with a radius of 60km around the village had turned to desert (figure C).

The traditional Rendille lifestyle had worked in balance with the environment. The new water supplies led to the exploitation of resources in a few limited areas, and the environment was damaged.

A **pastoral economy** or system is one in which:
- 50% or more households have an income from livestock or livestock-related activities
- milk or milk products make up at least 15% of the food and energy consumption of households.

B Rendille people herding camels

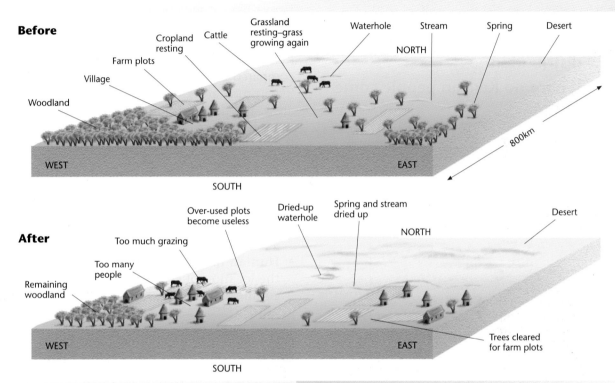

Before

Woodland
Village
Farm plots
Cropland resting
Cattle
Grassland resting–grass growing again
Waterhole
Stream
Spring
Desert
NORTH
800km
WEST
EAST
SOUTH

After

Remaining woodland
Too many people
Too much grazing
Over-used plots become useless
Dried-up waterhole
Spring and stream dried up
Desert
NORTH
Trees cleared for farm plots
WEST
EAST
SOUTH

C The process of desertification

FACT FILE

Oxfam working in the Wajir District

The main enemy in the Wajir District is drought. Nuria Hujaale is a Somali woman farmer who lives there. She lost all her animals in the drought of 1984. Oxfam gave her thirty goats to re-stock her herd. She recalls 'as soon as the goats arrived from Oxfam it began to rain. It was like a blessing.'

Twenty of the goats produced young within a year and within ten years the herd was over two hundred and fifty. Nuria was able to help other families with milk loans, but also sold some of her herd to buy camels, cows, clothes and food for the family. With the new prosperity families were able to survive the drought of 1992.

Nuria's family shares a homestead with five other families. It is surrounded by a fence of cut thorn that protects the people and animals in the homestead from attack by wild animals. Each family occupies one or two *herios*, domed houses made from arched branches, covered with mats of grass or palm. The door of each *herio* faces towards the thorn enclosure, which provides overnight housing for the family's goats. Close by are wigwams of sticks that safely pen the newborn kids.

The families in a homestead share the land and depend on each other for survival. These traditional relationships are enforced by the Islamic moral code, which encourages a redistribution of wealth.

3 PEOPLE AND SETTLEMENT

The distribution of population

▶ Where do people live in Kenya?

▶ What are the reasons for this distribution?

▶ Where do Kenyan people come from?

Kenya has a population of 29.7 million, according to the World Bank, which is just over half of the population of the UK. However, Kenya is twice the size in terms of land area compared with the UK. Most people in Kenya live in rural areas, and only 25% live in urban areas. The distribution of population is very uneven, with over 70% of the people concentrated on just 10% of the land (see map A).

The main factors affecting the distribution of population are:
- **Physical factors** – the amount and reliability of rainfall, suitable temperatures, altitude and soil fertility.
- **Human factors** – the history of **settlement**, the location of economic activities and communications.

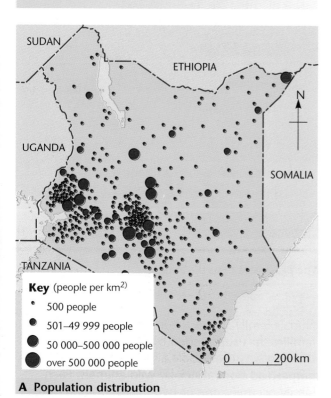

Key (people per km²)

- ° 500 people
- ● 501–49 999 people
- ● 50 000–500 000 people
- ● over 500 000 people

0   200 km

A Population distribution

C Medium density – Bamburi Beach, Mombasa

B High density – Muthare Valley, Nairobi

D Low density – Turkana nomadic pastoralists

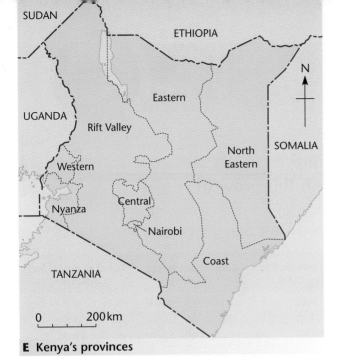

E Kenya's provinces

Physical factors

Most people in Kenya depend on **subsistence farming** for their survival or as their main source of income, so the settlement pattern is generally determined by the quality of the land and the suitability of the climate for agriculture. The following facts explain why the distribution of population is uneven:

- Two-thirds of Kenya cannot support a reasonable level of agricultural production.
- The north is too dry for growing crops, with low rainfall and poor groundwater supplies.
- Much of the south and east has unreliable rainfall, apart from a narrow coastal strip.
- The Kenyan Highlands have rich volcanic soils and a regular supply of rainfall.

FACT FILE

Kenya: a melting pot of races

Kenya's ethnic composition:

Kikuyu	21%
Luhya	14%
Luo	12%
Kalenjin	12%
Kamba	11%
Kisii	6%
Meru	5%
Mijikeda	5%
Maasai	2%
Turkana	1%
Embu	1%
Others (29 groups)	10%

Human factors

Kenya's history of settlement goes some way to explaining the distribution of people and the wide variety of cultures in the country. Recent history shows distinct periods of migration and settlement:

- 98% of Kenyans are Africans, and the majority belong to two major groups: the Bantu people who migrated from West Africa, and the Nilotic people from the Nile region to the north. These groups of people form distinct tribes, for example the Kikuyu. Most have settled in the Kenyan Highlands to the south and west of the country.
- Arab traders started coming to the Kenyan coast as far back as the ninth century. Trading settlements were established in the area of modern-day Mombasa, now a region of dense population. There are about 40 000 people living in Kenya of Arab origin.
- When the Europeans came to Kenya in the nineteenth century they settled in the best farming area on the Highlands to the south of the country. Settlers were attracted by the chance to start a new life in this rich farming area. The British settlers brought Asian workers in to build railways. Today, approximately 100 000 people of Asian origin live in Kenya: many are descendants of these early migrants.

Province	Population 1989	Density (per km²)
Central	3 284 800	249
Coast	1 904 100	23
Eastern	3 864 700	25
Nairobi	1 346 000	1884
North Eastern	554 000	4
Nyanza	3 892 600	311
Rift Valley	4 702 400	27
Wesern	2 535 900	308
Total	**22 084 500**	**39**

F Distribution of population by province

Two-thirds of Kenya's population are Bantu-speakers. The most numerous of these are the Kikuyu, the Luhya and the Kamba. Most other Kenyans are Nilotic-speaking. Those classed as Kenyan Asian, Arab and European number less than 1% of the total population, but they wield significant commercial power.

Population growth

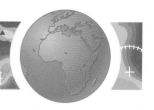

- ▶ How fast is Kenya's population growing?
- ▶ What are the problems connected with this growth?
- ▶ Can the growth be controlled?

Year	Birth rate /1000	Death rate /1000	Infant mortality rate/1000	Life expectancy (years)	Total population (millions)
1948	50	25	184	35	5.4
1962	50	19	174	44	8.6
1969	50	17	119	49	10.9
1979	54	14	84	53	15.3
1989	47	10	74	61	22.1
1995*	42	9	64	59	28.7
2000*	40	9	56	60	29.4

* Estimates from World Bank. All other figures from Kenya Censuses.

A Key population indicators, 1948–2000

Kenya's population is growing at a rate of 3.5% a year. This is less than it was (5%), but it still has one of the highest growth rates in Africa. Kenya's **natural increase** in population is above the average 2.3% growth rate for other LEDCs. In comparison, the UK's birth rate is 0.1%.

Changes in population size

Population growth is due both to natural increase, and to the fact that **in-migration** is greater than **out-migration**. Natural increase in population is the difference between the **birth rate** and the **death rate**.

Why is the natural increase in population so high in Kenya?

- Kenya is a mainly rural society and Kenyans need their children to help with work on the land.
- Parents are encouraged to have more children because infant mortality is so high – eight times the rate in the UK (64 per 1000 in Kenya, compared with 8 per 1000 in the UK).
- Over 50% of the population is under the age of 15 (24% in the UK). Kenyan girls traditionally marry young and have a longer time to bear children.

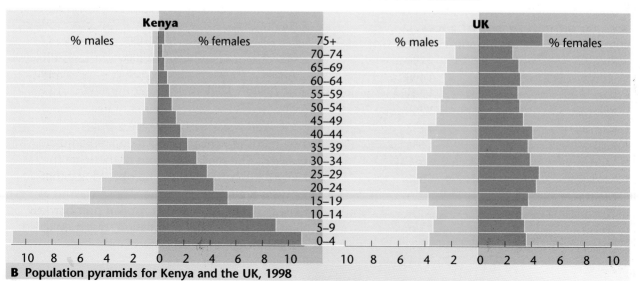

B Population pyramids for Kenya and the UK, 1998

- Many Kenyan women have limited access to education, and they do not always have an independent choice in deciding how many children they want to have.
- The cost of **contraception** is high, particularly in rural areas.
- **Life expectancy** is increasing owing to improving health care, safe water supplies and improved nutrition.

Problems connected with a growing population

- With a growing number of young people, and older people living longer, the dependent population is increasing (figure **B**). This is the number of people who are dependent on others for an income. In Kenya children work from an early age and people do not usually retire when they are older. So the situation is different from that in most MEDCs, such as the UK (figure **B**).
- In a country with a limited amount of fertile land, the demands on the **resource capacity** – the amount that can be produced from the land – is being exceeded.
- It has been estimated that over 30 000 new jobs will be needed every year to keep the growing population in employment.
- Most Kenyans depend on wood as their main source of fuel. A growing demand will lead to further environmental problems, such as desertification (see page 14).

Controlling population growth

Kenya's Population Agency aims to reduce the population growth rate to 2.5%, by reducing birth rates. Family planning centres were introduced into the country in 1968, but progress has been slow, because there are many education and cultural issues to be overcome.

C A family planning centre, Kirinyaga District

FACT FILE

Family planning

Kenya became the first sub-Saharan country to adopt a national family planning programme in 1968. The Ministry of Health collaborates with voluntary, church and other non-governmental organizations in providing clinics and distributing family planning information. Family Health Field Educator networks were established in the 1970s. Although based at health centres, they spend most of their time visiting villages. But by the early 1980s there was still a low user rate of contraception. In response, the government set up further clinics and contraceptive distribution points, particularly in rural areas.

Women with primary education, in Kenya have higher fertility rates than those with no education, as a consequence of their basic awareness of hygiene. Women with secondary education have the lowest fertility rates, the result of education opening up career greater opportunities. Urban fertility is lower than rural fertility because of a greater knowledge of and access to contraception. Women's groups across Kenya have had the most measurable success in promoting the need for effective family planning.

(Adapted from *Choices, Challenges and Changes*, published by the Commonwealth Institute.)

Urbanization and city life

> ▶ Why are Kenya's urban areas growing?
> ▶ What are the problems associated with urban growth?

Although Kenya's population is still mainly rural, the process of **urbanization** is becoming significant. The urban population is growing at an average rate of 7% per year compared with a population growth rate of 3.8% for the country as a whole.

The main reasons for this rapid rate of urbanization are as follows:
- **Rural to urban migration**. Rural people are abandoning or being forced from their traditional rural ways of life and are increasingly moving to urban areas. The reasons why people make such a move are often described as 'push and pull factors'.

- **Increased birth rates**. It is usually young people who migrate to the cities in search of new opportunities. Most migrants to city areas in Kenya are under the age of 30. These migrants are more likely to be of child-bearing age. The **fertility rate** for Kenyan women between 1990 and 1995 was estimated to be 6.8 (for British women the figure is 1.8). So cities grow fast if the birth rate is high.
- **Improved quality of life**. As living conditions and health care improve, life expectancy increases. It is usually in urban areas that the benefits are seen first.
- **International migration**. Kenya is seen as a land of opportunity for people from both LEDCs and MEDCs. Migrants coming into the country are usually attracted to urban centres. In recent years Kenya has had to cope with a huge number of refugees. In 1992 it was estimated that there were 400 000 refugees, compared with only 12 400 in 1990. Most of these refugees come from Somalia, Ethiopia and Sudan. Many start off in refugee camps but later migrate towards the cities where they can find work.

Problems of urban growth

When settlements grow rapidly it is difficult for the government to keep up with the increasing demand for services. Many families arriving in urban centres moved in order to escape the poverty of rural areas. They often have few resources and many end up in the shanty

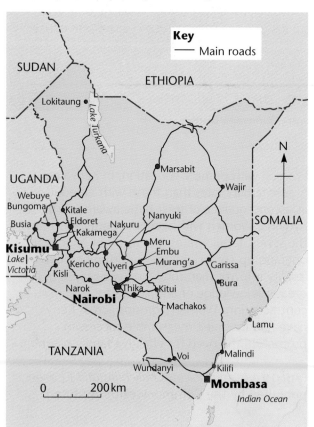

A Kenya's main towns

Year	Total population (millions)	Total population (millions)	Share (%)
1980	16.67	2.50	15
1990	22.75	4.03	17.7
2000	29.4	6.95	23.6
2010(est)	36.90	11.22	30.4

B Kenya's growing urban population

towns on the edges of Kenya's cities. Ziwa La Ng'ombe, Mombasa's largest shanty town, is home to 70 000 people. Residents of this **informal settlement** have no piped water supply so they are forced to buy drinking water. Diseases spread quickly, and health care provision is limited. Four out of five people in Ziwa La Ng'ombe are unemployed. Yet people continue to leave the rural areas in search of a new life in towns and cities. (See pages 24–25.)

C Nyeri, one of Kenya's fastest-growing centres

Push ...

- Farmers cannot earn enough money from farming their land to support their family.
- Farmland is divided up repeatedly amongst children so that after a few generations the plots become too small to support a family.
- There are few jobs in rural areas apart from farming, so anyone with an education does not stay.
- There are few services in rural areas: health care, education and transport facilities are limited.

Pull ...

- People believe there are greater employment opportunities in cities.
- Young people are attracted by the opportunities they see in the cities.
- Amenities such as health care and schools are usually better.

D Push and pull factors

FACT FILE

A growing drift to the cities

Many of the families in the larger towns and cities of Kenya have been driven off their land. Oxfam tries to give these families some hope and support as they drift into the shanty town areas. One of the unforeseen problems in rural displacement is conflict between different tribes. Recent problems have arisen because of land distribution in multi-ethnic areas. The government has tended to partition provinces and districts on an ethnic basis, a policy that promotes tribal differences.

Alice is a farmer driven from her home in Kaptarat, in May 1994.
'It was just after midnight. The men had stayed awake. They saw fires burning in different directions. Houses were being burnt. We went closer to the trading centre to be safe, and the men went to fight. But the warriors were many and well armed. Some of the men had arrow injuries, especially in their hands and legs, and in their bodies. My own house was burned. The police gave us a safe way out: we had been defeated.

'Before, we shared livestock. We went to each other's weddings and funerals. We didn't feel like different tribes. We would forgive them, but it is difficult to forgive a neighbour who is wearing your clothes and milking your cows.'

(Extract from Oxfam's *Kenya – a promised land?*)

Nairobi, Kenya's capital city

▶ **Where is Nairobi situated?**

▶ **Why was this site chosen?**

"Now a United Nations headquarters city, Nairobi is the economic centre of much of east and central Africa as well as Kenya. It continues to grow at an astonishing speed and with great energy if, at times, seemingly without control. In some areas Nairobi still looks and feels like an afterthought."
Spectrum Guide to Kenya

Nairobi is the capital city of Kenya. It has a population of 2.1 million – about 36% of Kenya's urban population. The city is some 500km inland from the coast. It is unusual to have a capital city so far inland in a coastal LEDC. Nairobi hasn't always been the capital: it succeeded Mombasa as Kenya's first city in 1907.

Nairobi's location can be traced back to the period of British settlement in the early 1900s. In 1896, the British started building a 935km railway to connect Mombasa on the coast with Lake Victoria. The railway was planned to open up Kenya and the bordering East African countries for trade through the Kenyan coastal ports. Construction started from Mombasa, and at the '317 mile marker post' a supply base was built. Here the land was flat, with a good supply of water. This settlement was named 'Ewaso Nairobi', a Maasai term for 'cool water'. This early railway town marked the beginnings of Nairobi.

Today, Nairobi lies on the intersection of the Great North Road (from Cape Town to Cairo) and the Trans-Africa Highway (Mombasa to Lagos). This has placed the city at a focal communication point in Africa. Nairobi has grown into an important political and commercial centre, both in Kenya and East Africa, and on a global scale. It is now the world headquarters of the United Nations Environment Programme.

A Location of Nairobi in Kenya

B Nairobi city centre: "Trees and gardens are more distinctive features than its towering skyline of concrete." *Insight Guide*

Contrasts in Nairobi

Nairobi is a truly **cosmopolitan** city. It marks the meeting point of several different tribal lands, although the Kikuyu are its largest group of residents. There are also a large number of Europeans and Asians.

"You can walk down mainstreet Nairobi and in ten minutes pass people representing almost every major language type in Africa and every other continent – and they could all be Kenyan citizens."
Insight Guide

A green city

The high-rise buildings in the centre of Nairobi look like any other modern city in the world, but the skyline is remarkably green and

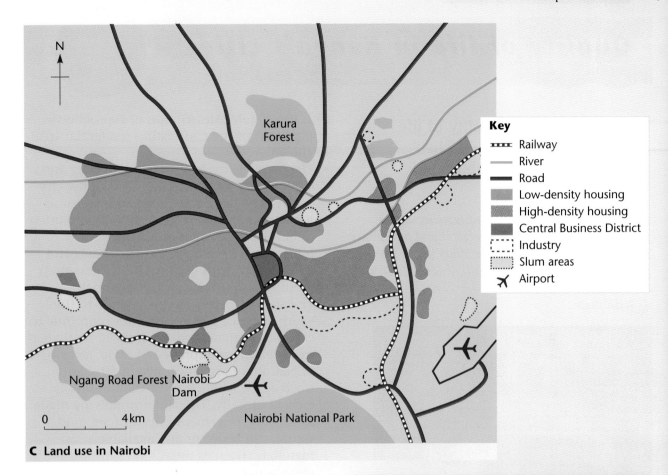

C Land use in Nairobi

Key
- ▭▭▭ Railway
- ── River
- ── Road
- Low-density housing
- High-density housing
- Central Business District
- Industry
- Slum areas
- ✈ Airport

includes large areas of trees and gardens. These were planted by the first settlers in an attempt to provide shade.

The City Park (Karura forest) to the north is the remains of an ancient forest and has been preserved for recreational use. To the south lies a 113km² wildlife park or 'wilderness suburb' where free-ranging wild animals live.

Year	Population
1901	8000
1925	30 000
1933	51 000
1948	119 000
1957	222 000
1969	509 000
1978	818 000
1989	1 346 000
1993	1 400 000
1998	2 100 000

D Nairobi's population growth

FACT FILE

Nairobi: a city of contrasts.

Nairobi is one of the largest capital cities in Africa. Yet, unlike most coastal African countries, Kenya's capital lies inland, far away from the coast. Its central business district is dominated by well-known multi-national names, many of them reflecting strong links with the UK – Barclays Bank, Norwich Union and British Airways. Centrally located services also reflect Nairobi's growing dependence on the tourist industry. There are many banks, money exchangers, travel agents, top hotels and galleries.

Before Independence, residential areas in Nairobi were segregated strictly on the basis of race. To the west lie the suburbs of Langata and Karen, where Europeans built homes. To the north are the hillside estates of Runda, Loresho, Muthaiga and Spring Valley. It is in these areas and in the expanding shanty towns wedged between the city centre and the growing suburbs that the less wealthy citizens, predominantly Kenyan Africans, live.

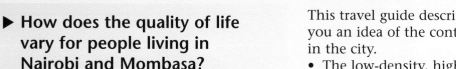

Quality of life in Kenya's cities

▶ How does the quality of life vary for people living in Nairobi and Mombasa?

"The suburbs run the gamut of housing design, from tin shacks in the truly decrepit and dangerous slums, to replicas of European villas in the smart suburbs of Muthaiga, a 'careful' distance from the city centre."

AA Pocket Guide

A A high-class residential area in Nairobi

B A shanty town: Mathare, Nairobi

This travel guide description of Nairobi gives you an idea of the contrasting residential areas in the city.

- The low-density, high-quality housing areas are found to the north and west of the city centre. The houses are large and luxurious. Residents are usually professionals and often of European or Asian origin. Most households have black Kenyan maids and gardeners to tend the beautifully designed grounds and private swimming pools.
- The shanty town areas are located to the south and east of the city. These continue to expand as migrants move in from rural areas in search of an improved lifestyle. Over 40% of Nairobi's population live in 50 shanty town areas, where 80% of the housing is erected illegally. The better homes are made from stone or cement but most are mud, wattle, cardboard or any available scrap materials. There is usually no **sanitation** or clean water supply.

Most of my friends in Mathare, Nairobi's largest and poorest slum, survive without many of the things I take for granted. They do not have toilets, running water, electricity or a good pair of shoes. Working people in the slum are lucky if they can earn 60 Kenyan shillings (about US$1) a day. Crammed into one-room shacks with sheets hanging from the ceilings as room dividers, the families are large with five to ten children.

C From the *Observer Magazine*, 5 September 1999

D Mombasa

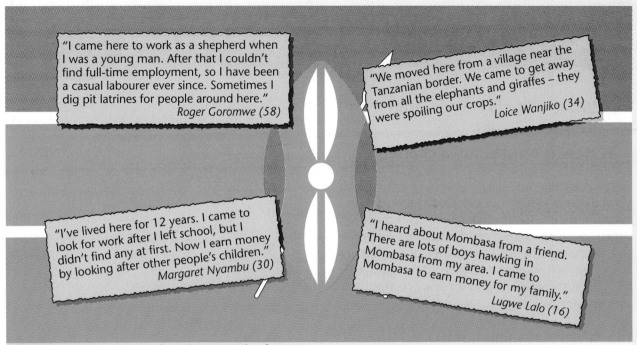

"I came here to work as a shepherd when I was a young man. After that I couldn't find full-time employment, so I have been a casual labourer ever since. Sometimes I dig pit latrines for people around here."
Roger Goromwe (58)

"We moved here from a village near the Tanzanian border. We came to get away from all the elephants and giraffes – they were spoiling our crops."
Loice Wanjiko (34)

"I've lived here for 12 years. I came to look for work after I left school, but I didn't find any at first. Now I earn money by looking after other people's children."
Margaret Nyambu (30)

"I heard about Mombasa from a friend. There are lots of boys hawking in Mombasa from my area. I came to Mombasa to earn money for my family."
Lugwe Lalo (16)

E Why some people moved to Ziwa La Ng'ombe

Mombasa

Mombasa is Kenya's second city and a major port serving both Kenya and the wider **hinterland** of other East African countries. Like Nairobi, Mombasa is a city of contrasts, with exotic buildings reflecting its past links with Arab traders, luxurious new buildings, and a sprawl of informal settlements or shanty towns on the edges of the city. Mombasa has grown rapidly in recent years, and between 70 and 80% of its residents live in the shanty town areas. People have moved in from other areas to find work and a better lifestyle (photo **D**). Many of the newcomers move into informal settlements like Ziwa La Ng'ombe on the outskirts of the city, 3km north of Mombasa Island.

Improving life in the shanty towns

Charities like ActionAid have been working in shanty town areas of Kenyan cities to try to improve the quality of life there. In Ziwa La Ng'ombe they work with women's and youth groups. Some of their activities are:

- Loans to women to start up a small business: when they make a profit they have more money to spend on other things.
- Training in skills of book-keeping and finance management helps in running a small business. Young people are trained in craft skills such as carpentry and plumbing.
- Community groups have been formed to identify changes needed, to draw up action plans and meet with local government departments.

FACT FILE

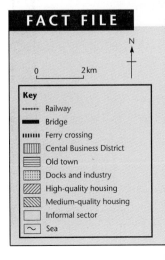

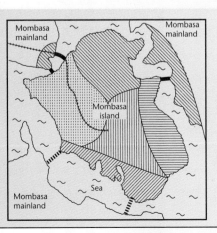

Key
- ┈┈┈ Railway
- ▬ Bridge
- ⅲⅲ Ferry crossing
- ▦ Cental Business District
- ▤ Old town
- ▨ Docks and industry
- ▧ High-quality housing
- ▨ Medium-quality housing
- ☐ Informal sector
- ∼ Sea

The map shows the different types of land use in the city of Mombasa.

Kaptalamwa, a village in Kenya

▶ **What is life like in a traditional Kenyan village?**

▶ **How is Kaptalamwa changing?**

Kaptalamwa still has many traditional village characteristics, partly because of its remote location. It is situated on the eastern side of the Cherangani Hills to the west of the rift valley and close to the border with Uganda. It lies at 2900 metres above sea level in the Elgeyo Maraket region.

Kapatalamwa is well sited as a local village and service centre for its 1500 inhabitants. Many of them are subsistence farmers who live and work on **shambas** (see page 32) surrounding the settlement. The main advantages of the site are:

- There is good access to spring water. There are no piped water supplies in the village. Women are responsible for collecting water each day.
- It is in a sheltered position above marshy ground on the valley floor, to avoid flooding. Being at a higher altitude the climate is cooler and wetter. It is above the level where mosquitoes breed, so it is free from **malaria**.

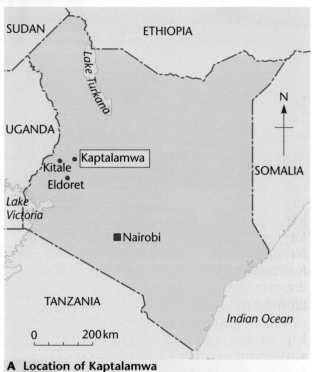

A Location of Kaptalamwa

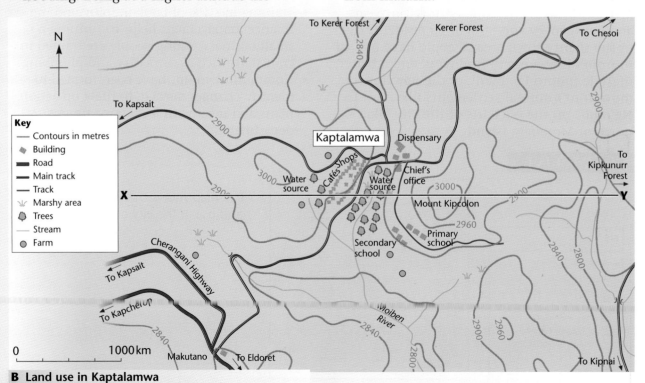

B Land use in Kaptalamwa

- It is close to the main Cherangani Highway which was funded by foreign aid. This is important as it connects the village with the larger centres of Eldoret and Kitale. These provide the people of Kaptalamwa with **higher-order services** such as banks, a post office, shops and hotels. The journey to these centres is by *matatu* – small vehicles that serve as a local bus service.

Services in the village

The main occupation in Kaptalamwa is subsistence farming, but many farmers also have a second job, or they grow **cash crops** to supplement their income. The village has carpenters, a shoemaker, builders and a few shops and cafés. There are a few government jobs including teachers, policemen, nurses and forest rangers. This area has retained much of its forest and natural vegetation – most of the forests are government-owned. There is also a dispensary in the village which deals with minor illnesses, and a doctor visits once a month.

Kaptalamwa has a primary and a secondary school. School attendance is not compulsory in Kenya. Those who do attend are charged fees for tuition, and must pay for books and uniforms. Children travel a long way, usually on foot, from the surrounding shambas, to attend school in Kaptalamwa. There are about 350 pupils in nine classes in the primary school. There is a secondary school next to the primary school. Children have to pass an entrance exam to get into the secondary school. If they don't pass they are kept back in the last year of the primary school – so pupils of up to 16 or 17 may still be in primary school!

C A recent view of Kaptalamwa

Recent changes in Kaptalamwa

The average family has five children. With improved health care, family size is increasing. New huts are being built for the expanding population. These are usually the traditional round huts built with local materials. Recently, some families have built their homes with locally gathered stones instead of the traditional mud walls. The grass-thatched roofs are being replaced by metal roofs, a sign of growing prosperity.

Some of the cafés in the village have installed battery-run televisions which are very popular with local people. Adult education classes have been introduced to help people develop more efficient methods of farming and to improve their health.

As the population continues to expand, there will be less farmland available. Also, people with an education may want to move to find jobs elsewhere.

FACT FILE

Education in Kenya
Since Independence in 1963 the numbers of primary and secondary schools and universities in Kenya have increased. The government pays the teachers' salaries but parental contributions are expected to cover a third of the costs of primary education and two-thirds of secondary education. Over 80% of primary aged children attend school, but the number drops to 30% at secondary level. But these average figures hide the differences between rural and urban areas, and between attendance by boys and by girls.

In the north the average attendance rate at school is below 30%; the standards of school achievement are usually the lowest in the country. In the Khorof Harar primary school in the north-east, only three out of twenty-eight pupils who took their national leaving exam in 1998 were girls. Children living in the rich city areas often attend expensive private schools where many of the teachers are UK expatriates. The children sit exams from British examination boards.

4 ECONOMIC ACTIVITY

Agriculture

▶ **How important is agriculture to the Kenyan economy?**

▶ **Where are the main farming areas?**

▶ **What are the main types of farming?**

Agriculture is very important to Kenya's economy. As in many LEDCs, agriculture is Kenya's main industry.

- It employs over 80% of the workforce, compared with just 2% in the UK.
- It accounts for 26% (1998) of the **Gross National Product (GNP)** – that is, the amount of money the country earns in a year.
- Over 50% of export earnings comes from agricultural produce.
- It provides **staple foods** – maize, wheat, potatoes – for Kenya's growing population.
- Kenya is one of the world's main suppliers of tea, coffee and **horticultural produce**.

Kenya has a land area twice the size of the UK, yet only 18% of it is suitable for agriculture. The main limitation is the climate – high temperatures and a low, unevenly distributed rainfall. This type of land is classed as having low agricultural potential. Good farming land is mostly found in the higher, well-watered south of the country. Nairobi, Mombasa and other large settlements are located here, but this further reduces the amount of productive land. It also means that in this area **intensive farming** has become important – that is, the greatest use is made of every piece of land. On the less productive land, larger areas are needed to support fewer people. Farmers here farm the land to feed their families with little surplus for sale. This is called **extensive subsistence farming**.

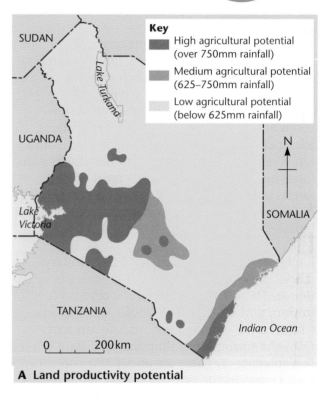

Key

■ High agricultural potential (over 750mm rainfall)

■ Medium agricultural potential (625–750mm rainfall)

□ Low agricultural potential (below 625mm rainfall)

SUDAN

Lake Turkana

UGANDA

Lake Victoria

SOMALIA

N

TANZANIA

Indian Ocean

0   200 km

A Land productivity potential

Subsistence farming

This type of farming accounts for more than half of all the agricultural produce in Kenya. Subsistence farms provide many Kenyan farmers and their families with staple food crops such as maize, wheat and vegetables. There are many of these smallholdings of between one and two hectares on the better farming land. It is farmed intensively to feed the large families. Some farmers also grow cash crops, such as tea and coffee, to bring in a cash income.

Some subsistence farmers, such as the Maasai, are nomadic pastoralists (see pages 32–33). They move their cattle to better grazing areas as the pastures become dry.

Commercial farming

The **commercial farms** are concentrated in the higher, cooler, well-watered areas to the south. Many of these are the large estates of over 750

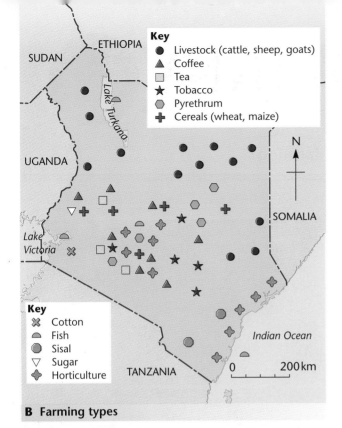

Key
- ● Livestock (cattle, sheep, goats)
- ▲ Coffee
- ☐ Tea
- ★ Tobacco
- ⬠ Pyrethrum
- ✚ Cereals (wheat, maize)

Key
- ✖ Cotton
- ⌂ Fish
- ◉ Sisal
- ▽ Sugar
- ✤ Horticulture

B Farming types

	Number	Average size
Smallholdings	1 700 000	2 hectares
Large farms and estates	3700	730 hectares

C Land ownership in Kenya

hectares and grow cash crops such as tea, coffee and flowers for export. There are good road, rail and air communications in these areas to transport the produce to markets quickly.

Commercial livestock farming, for example of cattle, is less important than crops. Yet it accounts for over half of the agricultural labour force and 10% of GNP.

Land ownership

Land ownership in Kenya is unequal. The smallholdings are owned by Kenyans, and over 54% of them are less than one hectare. The large estates are usually owned by people of European or Asian descent who first came to Kenya in the early 1900s.

FACT FILE

Land reform

In the early 1960s the 'Million Acres Scheme' resettled 34 000 Kenyan families on land previously set aside for Europeans. A further 100 000 hectares were redistributed between 1971 and 1976.

Under British rule, Africans had been forbidden or discouraged from growing coffee, tea and pyrethrum, which were the crops grown by settlers on large estates. But, by the early 1980s, smallholders were producing over 60% of Kenya's coffee and 40% of its tea. It is also the smallholders who produce most of Kenya's staple food products such as maize, which supplies almost half of the nation's calories and more than a third of its protein.

It was the European settlers who introduced the idea of land as a commodity to own. In the Kenyan sense land was a communal resource held in trust by the living for the benefit of future generations. 'Land belongs to a vast family of which many are dead, a few are living and countless members are still to be born' (quote by an African tribal leader).

Recently, however, growing populations and increased crop failures have forced many smallholders to sell out to larger farmers, often with absentee landowners. Though reliable figures are not available, it seems that more than one third of the best agricultural land is still owned by fewer than 1000 families or companies. This has resulted in a growing drift of landless farmers to the shanty town areas of cities and large towns in search of work.

There is also the increasing problem of using land to grow cash crops such as coffee and tea instead of the staple food crops that can feed the Kenyan people. With less staple crops being grown, Kenya is increasing dependent on imported crops, such as maize

Farmers are attracted by the income they receive from selling cash crops. However, the selling price on the world market is variable, depending on supply and demand. Small-scale farmers usually have a very limited profit margin compared with large multinational companies selling cash crops. Small farmers often lose out when trying to market their crops.

Changes in traditional farming

▶ **What are the traditional methods of farming?**

▶ **How are these changing?**

Despite the large amount of income from cash crops sold on the world market, most farms in Kenya grow food for local people. Traditional Kenyan farmers have adapted their farming styles to suit a variety of climates and environments. The most productive farms are those on the better farmland in the higher area to the west of the Great Rift Valley. Further north, in the arid lands, farming is less productive. However, the traditional styles of farming are under threat.

Shambas

'Shamba' is the name given to the small-holdings located on the higher, cooler area to the west of the Great Rift Valley. Each one consists of a few buildings in a compound surrounded by small fields. The fertile volcanic soils have been further improved by adding **humus** from the natural woodlands of the area. The climate is suitable for growing crops all year round and the land is farmed intensively. Most of the farms are 1–2 hectares, and support a family of 8–10 people with staple crops (maize, potatoes and vegetables). Goats, cattle and chickens are also kept to supplement the diet. This is subsistence farming. If there are any surplus crops, these are sold or exchanged at local markets. Traditional farming is **labour intensive**, and only basic hand tools are used.

In recent years these traditional farmers have begun to grow cash crops, such as tea. This provides useful extra income. However, there are problems threatening this lifestyle:

- As the population increases, particularly in rural areas, there is a growing demand for more staple foods.
- The success of the cash crop market encourages farmers to plant more cash crops and less staple crops.
- Many young people, particularly young men, are leaving the traditional lifestyle and moving to the cities.

A A typical shamba

The Maasai

The Maasai are a proud warrior tribe who have practised the same traditional methods of agriculture for thousands of years. The Maasai are pastoralists – that is, they graze their cattle on the drier savanna grasslands. They practise extensive agriculture by grazing few animals over a wide land area. They are semi-nomadic and move their cattle during the long dry season to find new grazing areas. The Maasai are traditionally subsistence farmers practising a sustainable lifestyle.

Until recently, the Maasai lived in small villages consisting of 30–50 basic huts made of local materials. Cow dung mixed with mud and grass is used to line the walls, the roofs are grass thatch, and there are no windows or chimneys. These are surrounded by a thick hedge to keep the cattle in at night and wild animals out.

Now, the Maasai lifestyle is changing. Many families are being forced to abandon their traditional farming methods. Wildlife parks are

C Lake Amboseli in the Amboseli National Park

B A threatened lifestyle? This Maasai farmer has sold his large cattle herd, preferring money to status

seen as a big threat to nomadic grazing. The Maasai have been evicted from many of their traditional grazing lands, for example around Lake Amboseli in the Amboseli National Park (photo C). The Park authorities see the Maasai lifestyle as a threat to the wildlife that is protected within the parks.

Many of those people who were evicted were given a small plot of land on which to grow staple food and cash crops rather than graze their cattle. Often the plots are not sufficient to provide enough food for the growing population. People need to earn money to pay for their children to be educated in local

schools. Some improvements have been provided to compensate the displaced tribes: better housing with piped water supplies, and better health facilities. The people make some income from work in the game reserves, but the traditional warrior race is fast disappearing.

One way forward is through the tourist industry. The Kenyan Wildlife Service has been negotiating with the Maasai who were evicted from Amboseli National Park in 1973. They lost some 250km^2 of their former grazing land.

A spokesman for the Maasai said:
"I believe the future of Amboseli Maasai lies more with wildlife tourism and pastoralism than it does with dryland cultivation and pastoralism. Tourism will bring employment to the area, and if the hotels and tour operators only employed local people, this would have a big impact on the community's decision to allow tourism."

FACT FILE

Warriors fight for a fairer future

After years of failing to profit from safari tourists, Africa's Maasai tribe have begun to take control. The Kisongo people have established a conservation area, Eselenkei, on their own land and on their own terms. Eselenkei Wildlife Park is the result of years of planning and political activity. Esenlenkei nestles up against the Amboseli Wildlife Park in the so called 'dispersal area', where during the rainy season much of Amboseli's wildlife saunters through. Roads have been painfully cleared by hand, using just farm tools. Waterholes have been dug to make sure wildlife stays there once the rainy season ends.

The accommodation tents are luxurious with hot showers, copper basins, wooden wardrobes, comfortable beds and solar-powered electric lights. Everything is 'low-impact': take it all down and you would never know a camp had been there. The food served is not the traditional Maasai style – cow's milk with fresh blood. Instead, meals like roast chicken and lasagne are provided to cater for other tastes. However, it might well be served by a (usually) semi-nomadic Maasai warrior wearing traditional red robes and multicoloured beaded jewellery, sword dangling at his side. The costumes aren't put on for the tourists, it's just the way they dress. (*Observer*, 9th April 2000.)

Growing tea in Kenya

▶ Why does Kenya grow so much tea?
▶ What advantages and disadvantages does tea-growing bring to the people of Kenya?

A Logo of the Tea Board of Kenya

Kenya became the world's leading exporter of tea for the first time in 1996, ahead of Sri Lanka and India. One-third of all the tea exported from Kenya goes to the UK.

Tea is Kenya's main cash crop and ranks second only to tourism as an earner of foreign income. It brings in about 28% of the total export earnings, worth US$350 million in 1995. The tea industry is labour intensive and employs over one million Kenyans.

Tea-growing and marketing are regulated by the Tea Board of Kenya (**A**) which tries to get the best deal for its farmers. The Kenyan government levies a 1% tax on tea exporters for running the industry and marketing tea abroad.

Over 110 000 hectares of Kenya's best farmland are used for tea **plantations** (**B**). Many of these are owned by large **multinationals** like Brooke Bond. The tea-growing area is concentrated on the western side of the Great Rift Valley. This is an area of high agricultural potential (see map A on page 30). Tea

estates were introduced by European settlers in the early 1900s, who cleared the natural forest and replaced it with thousands of hectares of tea bushes.

This area is good for growing tea because:
• there is at least 1300mm rainfall each year;
• the soils are acid, well-drained and deep;
• the land is high, between 1000 and 2000 metres, which means temperatures are lower.

Half of the tea grown for export is grown by the many smallholders in the area. The other half is grown on a few large estates. Brooke Bond has an estate at a place called Kericho (**C**), and this alone produces 12% of Kenya's total tea output (257 million kilograms in 1996). With intensive methods of production, some of the larger estates produce 4000–5000kg per hectare (the world average is 1500kg/ha).

B A tea plantation

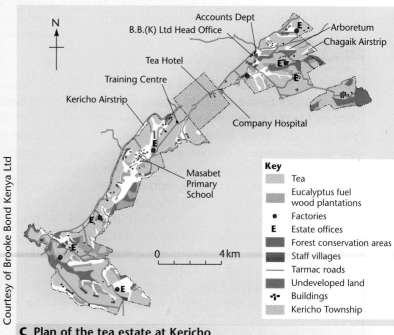

Courtesy of Brooke Bond Kenya Ltd

Accounts Dept
B.B.(K) Ltd Head Office
Arboretum
Chagaik Airstrip
Tea Hotel
Training Centre
Kericho Airstrip
Company Hospital
Masabet Primary School

Key
Tea
Eucalyptus fuel wood plantations
● Factories
E Estate offices
Forest conservation areas
Staff villages
Tarmac roads
Undeveloped land
Buildings
Kericho Township

0   4km

C Plan of the tea estate at Kericho

From the seed to the table

- Tea seedlings are grown in a sheltered nursery. After five months, the bushes are planted out in the fields. They grow to about a metre in height before the mature leaves can be plucked. By plucking the leaves at intervals of about 18 days, the bushes are kept at the same height. The plucking is done by hand; it is very labour intensive. Pluckers on large estates work a 7-hour day, earning KSh 360 (about £3.00) daily. There are also benefits: families have free housing, schools, health care and medical facilities.

- Once the tea is plucked it is dried for a day to lose 70% of its moisture content. The leaves are then crushed under large rollers and shredded. The tea is fermented by leaving it exposed to the air, and the leaves turn brown. Next they are fired in a stove to a temperature of 88°C and their water content is reduced to 2%. They are then sieved, graded and tasted before being packed for export.

- The problem for small tea growers is that they often get a low price for selling their tea as there is so much competition from different growers. The Tea Board helps protect their interests. The Fairtrade foundation (**D**) is negotiating with the smallholder tea organization (KDTA) to ensure better deals for growers.

D The Fairtrade logo

Annual production:	264 000 tonnes
Area under cultivation:	113 000 hectares
Annual income from exports:	US$300 million

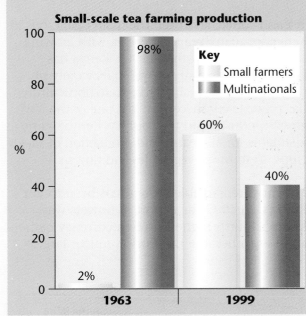

E Tea production in Kenya

FACT FILE

Fairtrade Foundation

The Fairtrade Foundation is an association of fair trader wholesalers, retailers and producers whose members are committed to providing fair wages and good employment opportunities to economically disadvantaged artisans and farmers worldwide. It directly links low income producers with consumer markets and educates consumers about the importance of purchasing fairly traded products which support living wages and safe and healthy conditions for workers in the Third World.

Fair trade works by:
- Reducing the number of 'middlemen' and overheads so that the profits go directly to the workers.
- Working with co-operatives that provide safe and dignified working conditions.
- Encouraging producers to reinvest profits into their communities.
- Shifting processing and packing activities to LEDCs to boost incomes (often these activities take place in MEDCs at present).
- Publicizing human human rights violations to consumers. This puts pressure on companies to do something about their working practices. Consumer pressure has forced many of the manufacturers of our top selling brands of fashion clothes to pass an internal code of conduct for its suppliers to ensure fair and humane treatment of its employers.

New cash crops – horticulture

▶ How important is horticulture to the economy?

▶ What are the costs and benefits of growing cash crops?

KENYA
FLOWER COUNCIL

A Logo of the Kenya Flower Council

1992	1993	1994	1995	1996	1997	1998
209	390	415	531	682	752	831

Source: *Ministry of Planning and National Development*

B Value of horticultural exports from Kenya, 1992–98 (KSh)

Tea and coffee have been the main cash crops in Kenya for many years. However, with growing competition from other LEDCs, Kenya has attempted to diversify or widen its variety of cash crops. Introducing large-scale horticulture has proved very successful. It is one of the few growth industries in the country. Kenya's climate is suitable for all-year-round production of salad crops, fresh fruits, vegetables and flowers.

The most remarkable growth has been in cut flowers. In 1999 the export of flowers was Kenya's fourth highest foreign currency earner, and Kenya became the world's fourth largest exporter of cut flowers. Two-thirds of the flowers go to Holland, mainly for re-export to other European countries. The Kenyan Flower

Chris Shaw and his family have worked the 80ha Celinoco farm since his grandfather started growing tea here in 1930. Most of the land is still planted with tea, but about 9ha have been replaced with flowers over the past five years. The farm lies 40km north-west of Nairobi on the edge of the Great Rift Valley, at a height of 2500m above sea level. The climate here is temperate with an average annual rainfall of 1050mm and average temperatures of 18°C.

Growing the flowers

Celinoco grows mainly Alstromeria flowers with a few summer varieties such as Delphinium. The Alstromeria are harvested all year round. Alstromeria are perennial plants and go on producing for about four years until they have to be replaced. The ground is then ploughed up and new seeds are sown. The flowers take about 4 months to grow. On average the Alstromeria will produce about 150–200 stems per square metre. Mr Shaw gets about 4.5 pence per stem. The flowers can be grown outdoors but grow best under shade nets which help keep them cool and damp in the hot weather. The farm also buys in a range of exotic species, which are then sold on.

C Celinoco Flower Farm

Council (figure A) regulates the growing and marketing of flowers and flower products.

Growing concerns

There are, though, growing concerns about the impact of introducing another cash crop, both on the Kenyan people and on the environment:

- The horticulture estates are concentrated on land that has a high potential for agriculture, so land that could be used to grow staple crops is being used for cash crops.
- With a rapidly growing population and two-thirds of the land unsuitable for agriculture, more pressure will be put on less land.
- Maize is Kenya's staple food crop. There is limited chance of further expansion. In 1996 thousands of tonnes of maize were imported from South Africa to keep up with growing demand.
- The attraction of a cash income encourages smallholders to grow less staple and more cash crops.
- The use of chemically-based pesticides and fertilizers is causing serious pollution problems.
- The increase in air traffic to transport the flowers is causing air and noise pollution.

FACT FILE

Tesco joins the Kenyan Flower Council.
Tesco, the largest retailer of flowers and plants in the UK, became an associate member of the Kenyan Flower Council earlier this year. Tesco has been selling houseplants for the last 19 years and flowers for the last 14 years. Customers are increasingly concerned about where, how and by whom their plants and flowers are grown. In order to meet their concerns, Tesco introduced a protocol called Nature's Choice. This covers four key areas: chemical use, protection of health, protection and enhancement of the environment and conservation of natural resources.
(Taken from the *Kenyan Flower Council Spring 2000 newsletter*.)

Find out more by e-mailing kfc@africaonline.co.ke or by visiting the website www.kenyaflowers.co.ke

The farm employs 100 people, but only 25% are permanent – the others are taken on as casual labour when they are needed.

Marketing
The UK is the fastest-growing market for Kenyan flowers. In 1998, Celinoco exported nearly 8 million stems of Alstromeria, most of these to Europe, including the UK. The high season for Europe is from September to May; during the remaining months the flowers go to South Africa and Australia. The flowers go to a number of different clients, including supermarket chains and smaller wholesalers who sell to smaller florists and garage forecourts.
Celinoco has one of the most advanced marketing networks in Kenya, selling to 30 clients in 12 different countries such as EU countries, Australia and South Africa. This cuts out all the middlemen and increases the profit margin. (Most other producers sell directly to Dutch auctions, so prices are variable.)

▶ Why is tourism important to Kenya?

"Kenya, unlike most other African countries, combines two major attractions for the visitor: superlative game viewing, and a beach holiday besides the Indian Ocean."
AA Guide

Kenya is a beautiful country and offers a huge variety of attractions to tourists. Tourism has given a major boost to the Kenyan economy in recent years. Like many other LEDCs, Kenya used to be dependent on the export of **primary products** such as tea, coffee, **pyrethrum** and other plantation crops. But two-thirds of the country is unsuitable for agriculture, and a growing population was becoming dependent on fewer sources of income.

Tourism is not new to Kenya. Sportsmen from the Western world have hunted in the country's rich game reserves since the early 1900s. More recently, visitors have been attracted to Kenya's sun-drenched beaches. In 1998, two-thirds of the 770 000 tourists to Kenya spent their holidays in the coastal resorts to the north and south of Mombasa. Tourism is now Kenya's biggest single foreign currency earner, and has overtaken tea: tourism now earns US$448 million and tea earns US$397 million. The tourist industry employs more than 100 000 Kenyans, in a range of jobs.

Tourist attractions

- Most tourists travelling to Kenya go there to experience a unique type of holiday. With its varied landscape, spectacular display of wildlife and pleasant climate, the country offers 'something for everyone'.
- Tourists on safari can view a wide range of wildlife at close quarters in some of the best game parks in the world.
- Mombasa and other coastal resorts offer white sandy beaches, coral reefs, palm trees and deep clear water.
- Communications are good, both internally and with other countries. Kenya Airways

Bamburi Beach Hotel

    Single saver

Location: Right by the sandy beach at Bamburi, about 8 miles north of Mombasa and 30 minutes from the airport.

Accommodation: 150 rooms, simply furnished with shower, air-conditioning, balcony or terrace with views of the grounds.

Facilities: Swimming pool, squash courts, fitness centre, windsurfing and snorkelling. There is also a dive centre and glass-bottom boat trips can be arranged. In addition to the main restaurant, there is a speciality restaurant (at a supplement), and a pool-side snack bar. There is some evening entertainment as well as the hotel's nightclub, and the hotel also has a small shop and beauty salon.

Opinion: A popular, lively medium-class hotel and extremely good value.

A Beach holiday

connects the major towns and tourist destinations with world-wide international airports.

- The climate varies from the hot sun-drenched beaches around Mombasa to the cooler areas at a higher altitude around Nairobi.
- Facilities and amenities in the hotels, game reserves and lodges are generally of a very

high standard (80% of major hotels have been established with foreign investment).

KENYA SAFARI (6 DAYS/5 NIGHTS)

DAY 1 • MAASAI MARA
Travel through the Great Rift Valley into the Maasai Mara, taking an afternoon game drive before spending the evening at Keekorok Lodge. Here you can enjoy a sunset stroll on the raised walkway overlooking a hippo pool before enjoying a drink in the cosy lounge. **Overnight:** Keekorok Lodge.

DAY 2 • MAASAI MARA
A full day to explore the plains of the Maasai Mara on morning and afternoon game drives. **Overnight:** Keekorok Lodge.

DAY 3 • TREETOPS
Head north into the cooler mountain scenery of the Aberdares. Lunch at Lake Naivasha before travelling on to a late check-in at your forest lodge on stilts, Treetops, renowned for its marvellous viewing platform. **Overnight:** Treetops.

DAY 4 • SAMBURU
Drive past majestic Mt Kenya and over the Equator en route to Samburu. Enjoy lunch followed by an afternoon game drive. Samburu Lodge nestles on the banks of the Uaso Nyiro River below a backdrop of jagged mountains. Relax in the popular Crocodile Bar overhanging the water, an ideal vantage point to watch the nightly crocodile feeding.
Overnight: Samburu Lodge.

DAY 5 • SAMBURU
A full day of morning and afternoon game drives in Samburu National Reserve where you may be lucky enough to spot giraffe or ostrich.
Overnight: Samburu Lodge.

DAY 6 • NAIROBI
Cross the Equator once more on your return to Nairobi.

Inclusions: 5 nights' accommodation
- game drives as indicated
- meals as indicated.

Tour departs: Nairobi Sunday approx 8am, returns Nairobi Friday approx 12pm.

Please note: no children under 10 yrs.

B On safari

FACT FILE

Alternative attractions
The Kenyan Government is keen to develop alternative venues for tourism. It hopes to reduce the detrimental impact of visitors and the infrastructure developed for them, at the most visited spots. Newer areas to be promoted include some of the driest areas of Kenya. One of the proposed ideas is to establish health spas. Kenya has plenty of geothermal springs, the most significant of which are around Lake Bagoria and Lake Baringo, 345km from Nairobi.

Further projects include the extension of the number of golf courses (there are already thirty-six), promoting cruises on Lake Victoria, and the building of conference centres to attract a more regular trade of business travellers. Several companies are now promoting two-nation vacations, which might combine rafting down the Nile River in Uganda or a visit to the Seychelles with a Kenyan safari trip.

Increasing the number of tourist venues may bring job and investment opportunities to a wider range of people and regions in Kenya. However, there are the possible negative impacts that may cause damage to ecosystems, cultures and local traditions. There will also be a need for major investments to improve the road and communication systems between the central areas of Kenya and more remote locations.

Advantages and disadvantages of tourism

► What benefits has tourism brought to Kenya?
► What problems has tourism caused?

The advantages
Tourism has given a major boost to the economy and brought many advantages to Kenya:
- Tourism provides both direct and indirect employment for over 100 000 people. **Formal employment** includes direct employment in hotels and other tourist facilities. Indirect employment is created in the construction industry and agriculture. **Informal employment** opportunities are created for workers in the craft industries and for street vendors.
- Development in communications by road, rail and air have brought benefits to the whole country. Local roads have been improved and the telephone system has been extended.
- Tourism is the single highest export earner for the country. In 1998 Kenyan tourism earned KSh 17 500 million. Income for individuals and the government has meant that people can enjoy a better quality of life.
- Services such as hospitals and public utilities like electricity supplies have been improved to cater for tourists, and local people can also benefit from these.
- Resources such as wildlife are protected in order to continue to attract tourists – the tourist industry must be sustainable.

The disadvantages
Kenya has been able to diversify its economy through tourism. However, the tourist industry also brings problems:

- It can damage local environments and cultures. Cultural traditions may be changed so that they can be performed for the tourists.
- The industry is sensitive to bad publicity, and tourist numbers dropped during the 1990s as a consequence. For example, in 1998 violence broke out in the coastal resorts near Mombasa and as a result the number of German tourists visiting Kenya dropped by 20%.
- Behaviour by tourists (for example inadequate or inappropriate dress) may offend local people.
- About 80% of the major hotels on the coast – two-thirds of those in Nairobi and at least two-thirds of the lodges in the national parks – are either completely or partly owned by foreign investors. This means that many of the profits leave the country.
- Although many people are employed by the tourist industry, Kenyans often get the low-paid, low-skilled jobs such as cleaners and porters. Tourism has created many opportunities for the informal sectors of employment, but this has led to a growth in crime, prostitution, and clashes with the police.

The way forward
Tourism must be seen as a sustainable industry if it is to continue to prosper and bring benefits for the Kenyan people. **Ecotourism** – that is, tourism that encourages people to come and appreciate the natural environments without causing any damage to them – is

1992	14 260
1993	24 440
1994	28 100
1995	24 100
1996	24 160
1997	22 640
1998	17 500

A Income from tourists (KSh million)

Country	Thousands	%
Germany	1276	25.2
UK	934	18.5
Kenya residents	783	15.5
Switzerland	302	6.0
France	278	5.5
USA	233	4.6
Italy	175	3.5

B Main sources of Kenya's tourists

Tourism has had a significant impact on people living in Mombasa, where ActionAid works. The construction of runways at Moi International Airport caused the eviction of large numbers of people from their homes. From 1975 to 1979, when the airport was finished, these people were forced to move to Ziwa La Ng'ombe, an area to the north of Mombasa Island (see page 27). Residents of Ziwa La Ng'ombe have been affected by tourism in other ways, too. They used to have direct access to the sea for fishing, but with privatization of land and beach fronts for the construction of hotels, the sea is no longer accessible. As the residents of Ziwa La Ng'ombe say, "Other people have coffee and wildlife for local income generation. We used to have the sea as a natural gift, but not any more."

C A case study from ActionAid

becoming important in Kenya. However, many people are concerned about the impact of spreading tourism to new areas of the country. Some **indigenous** tribes are particularly concerned about this (extract **D**).

"Most of all it is our culture we must protect. Before the people will agree to opening up our land for wildlife tourism, thereby changing so radically our farming habits and risking our livelihood, it must be made clear how the negative impacts will be overcome by the positive ones. If we can be sure we will be better off by changing then we will welcome tourism."

D David Lovatt Smith, a former warden of Amboseli Park, *People and the Planet* (Vol.6, No.4), 1997

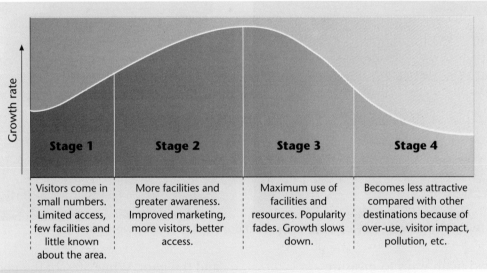

E Tourism as an industry: cycles and stages

Stage 1	Stage 2	Stage 3	Stage 4
Visitors come in small numbers. Limited access, few facilities and little known about the area.	More facilities and greater awareness. Improved marketing, more visitors, better access.	Maximum use of facilities and resources. Popularity fades. Growth slows down.	Becomes less attractive compared with other destinations because of over-use, visitor impact, pollution, etc.

FACT FILE

Ecotourism in Kenya

Ecotourism is sustainable, low impact tourism which benefits local communities and provides opportunities for these communities to have some direct control over local tourism. Conservationists and private sector operators give professional advice and support to these ventures. In Kenya ecotourism is a new venture and has already met with some obstacles. There have been some problems of conflict over land, particulary where land borders wildlife reserves which already have established tourist industries.

However, there are several success stories.

The Kuku Field Studies Centre is located 225km south of Nairobi. It was established to offer cultural and environmental educational opportunities to students of all ages and nationalities. All money earned from the centre is used for educational purposes and for community projects which benefit the Maasai members of the Kuku Group Ranch. Kuku is a model for financially self-sustainable environmental education in Africa.

5 DEVELOPMENT, TRADE AND AID

Development

▶ How can you measure development?
▶ How developed is Kenya?

A Different levels of economic development – street vendors and city office workers

There are two main ways to measure development: by the economy or wealth of a country, and by its social development or the quality of life of its people.

Measuring economic development

One measure of economic development is **Gross National Product (GNP) per head**, or the amount of money a country earns in a year, divided by the number of people in the country. Kenya has a GNP per head of US$353 (1998), which makes it the 22nd poorest country in the world. However, measuring a country's development by its GNP alone hides several important factors:

- **Inequalities** – in many LEDCs such as Kenya, wealth remains with a few people. Kenya is the second most unequal country in the world after Brazil, with a huge gap between the rich and the poor. While 50% of the population (almost 14 million) exist on less than US$1 a day, the top 10% of the population earn 47% of the country's income.
- **Informal employment** – many Kenyan people have informal jobs, e.g. street vendors. Money is exchanged without records, so does not appear in the GNP figures.
- **Subsistence lifestyles** – 80% of the Kenyan population are employed in farming. Many are subsistence farmers who live off what they eat, and their earnings are not recorded.
- GNP focuses on money and ignores people's quality of life.
- GNP compares Kenya's income with that of other countries but does not take into account the local value of the currency or how much it will actually buy. This is called the adjusted income per capita.

Country	GNP per capita (US$)	Life expectancy	Birth rate per 1000	Death rate per 1000	Adult literacy per 1000	HDI (1 = highest)
Kenya	353	57 years	31	15	78%	0.48
UK	18 700	79 years	13	11	99%	0.92
USA	26 980	79 years	15	9	99%	0.93
Japan	36 640	83 years	10	8	99%	0.94
Uganda	190	53 years	52	14	41%	0.33
Tanzania	100	56 years	50	13	36%	0.36
India	290	61 years	31	10	50%	0.44

B Social development in selected countries

Measuring social development

Social development indicators give a better idea of the quality of life experienced by people but do not give a clear picture of the inequalities. Social indicators measure health, education and social welfare. The United Nations Development Programme has drawn up the Human Development Index (HDI), which is a composite measure of social indicators. It includes factors such as life expectancy, **literacy**, infant mortality and access to health care. Kenya has made great advances in health care, primary education and female literacy. Infant mortality has come down to 67 per 1000, and life expectancy is now 61 for women. However, high birth rates continue to put pressure on limited resources. The United Nations ranks Kenya 136th out of 173 countries in the world in terms of the HDI.

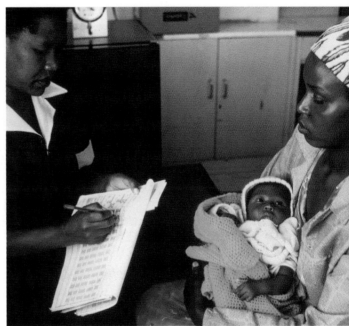

C A nurse checks a newborn baby at a health care centre in Machakos

FACT FILE

Finding the correct solution to rural development in Kenya

Power for women
Women are responsible for the majority of work in rural areas and need power in terms of land rights and educational equality in order to develop the skills to bring about change in rural areas.

Respecting local culture
Local people have adapted to the conditions of the climate and terrain. This local knowledge should be used in decision-making about future change.

Appropriate technology
The technology used should be appropriate to the skills, resources and finances of the local people.

Preserving the environment
A healthy environment is essential to long-term sustainable agriculture.

Meeting basic needs
Development should start with tackling the problems people face day-to-day in order to establish a secure basis for the future.

Self-reliance
Outside agencies have often thought that they need to 'show the way'; however, it is the local people who know their own needs and by becoming involved, gain the pride and confidence needed if a project is to succeed.

Productive in the long term
As well as working towards meeting the immediate needs, a development project must look towards a better future.

Resiliant to change
A development project must accommodate changes, both climatic and political.

43

Economic change

▶ **What problems face Kenya's economy?**

▶ **What is the government doing to improve the economy?**

A Kenya's two-speed economy

"What strikes a visitor to Kenya's capital is the huge number of contrasts. As in many African nations, there are glassy high-rise buildings housing multinational firms and diplomats, but just a stone's throw away you find the street children as well. There are at least 2 million unemployed, 25% in urban areas, and an estimated 10 million living in poverty out of a population of 25 million."

Quote from the Courier Country Report No.157

Kenya has the fastest-growing economy in East Africa, with an annual GNP growth rate of 5% in 1995 (2.8% in 1998). The government aims to turn Kenya into one of the world's **newly industrializing countries** (NICs) by 2020, hoping for the same economic success as the Asian NICs have enjoyed. However, Kenya has many problems typical of many other LEDCs:

- Kenya has a huge **trade deficit**. This has been partly offset by loans from international institutions such as the World Bank and the International Monetary Fund. However, these loans have conditions attached to them and may be withdrawn.
- Kenya has huge overseas debts. In 1998 it had an external debt of US$7.4 billion. Paying back the debt and interest takes the equivalent of 25% of all export earnings.

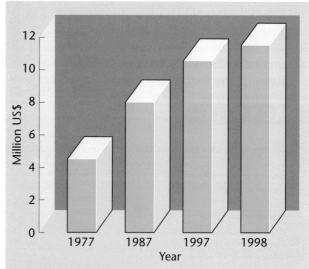

B GNP growth, 1977–98

- Kenya's exports are mainly primary products which are at risk from changes in world prices. Kenya's biggest export earner is tourism, but this can also be vulnerable to change. In 1992 tourism made up 29% of Kenya's total export receipts, but in 1998 this dropped to 24% after cancellations due to bad publicity.
- The **World Trade Organization**'s aims to **liberalize** trade will affect Kenya and many other countries. They will lose trade support and guaranteed markets. Kenya's own industries have been affected – for example,

cheap textile imports have forced the closure of textile factories because local manufacturers cannot compete.

- There is a huge gap in income levels between Kenyan people. Most (80%) of the workforce is employed in agriculture, many at subsistence level. More manufacturing industry is needed to create a wider range of jobs.

The way forward?

The Kenyan government has drawn up a series of economic development plans, which aim to increase employment, especially in manufacturing:

- To privatize more government-owned industry and to attract more outside investment. In 1996 Kenya had 700 medium and large-scale industries, 200 of which were owned by multinationals based in Britain, the USA, Germany and the Far East.

- To encourage **import substitution** of some products. Maize is Kenya's most important staple crop, yet thousands of tonnes are imported from South Africa every year. The government aims to increase Kenya's own production by using fertilizers and more efficient farming methods.

- The government hopes to increase employment rates in rural areas by developing labour-intensive **agro-industries**.

- The government has reduced taxes and regulations on imports and exports. It is encouraging exports of higher-value exotic products and more manufactured goods. Part of this scheme involves setting up Export Processing Zones (EPZs) (figure **C**).

- Athi River Export Processing Zone in Nairobi was established in 1993. Among other factories, Equitea Ltd, a Kenyan tea company, has located here, creating 40 jobs.

- Kenya-Rafiki EPZ on the Nairobi–Thika highway was established in 1996. This has seven factory zones, to be leased to foreign and local investors, and over 1000 new jobs have been created.

- Mombasa EPZ, established in 1994, is on the coast just 18km north of Mombasa. Livingstone Teas, part of the Equitea group, has set up a processing and packing unit here. The location provides easy access to the port for export.

By 1997 there were 15 EPZs in Kenya, with 82 local and foreign companies established there.

HOST COUNTRY

Provides:
- workers
- services (electricity, water, transport)
- buildings

Gains:
- wages
- experience
- payment for services
- buildings

EXPORT PROCESSING ZONE

FOREIGN COMPANIES

Provide:
- raw materials
- partly finished goods
- technology
- capital
- management

Gain:
- finished products
- profits

C Export Processing Zones

FACT FILE

Private investment boosts for Kenya

The Kenyan government is gradually releasing its state-owned industries to private investors as a way of improving many of its loss-making ventures.

Kenyan Airways was privatized in 1992 and transformed from an almost bankrupt industry into one of the most successful airlines in the world. The Dutch airline KLM invested over $26 million in the company in 1996. The air industry is a huge growth industry in Kenya, directly related to the growth in tourism and horticulture.

Kenyan Post and Telecommunications have set out to attract private investment locally and from overseas. The state-owned company's aim is to improve the 1997 provision of 0.16 lines to 1 line for every 100 people in rural areas and from 4 lines to 20 lines per 100 people in urban areas by the year 2015. They estimate this will mean the installation of an extra 2.7 million lines costing $270 million annually. The government realizes that it cannot keep up with the cost of the rapidly increasing demand for telephone links and other technologies without the involvement of foreign giants such as AT&T and British Telecom.

International trade

- ▶ How important is trade to Kenya?
- ▶ Which countries does Kenya trade with?
- ▶ What are Kenya's main imports and exports?

A Some of Kenya's exports – flowers, tourism and coffee

Like most countries, Kenya depends on trade for its economic growth. Trade is the movement of goods and services between countries. Very few, if any, countries are self-sufficient and can provide all they need; they have to buy or import goods and services from other countries. Some countries have a **comparative advantage** over others in producing goods. For example, Kenya's tropical climate, fertile soils and historical links with the British give it a comparative advantage as the world's main exporter of tea.

Like many other LEDCs, Kenya has built its trade on exporting a few primary products such as tea and coffee. These raw materials are usually processed, packed and marketed in other countries. The UK buys most of Kenya's tea and Germany buys most of its coffee. But the real profit from most primary products is made from selling finished, processed items.

In turn, Kenya imports high-value manufactured goods from MEDCs. The gap between the value of imports and exports is called the **trade balance**:

- If a country's exports have a higher value than its imports it has a trade surplus.
- If a country's imports have a higher value than its exports it has a trade deficit.

Kenya has a large trade deficit. For example, the value of imports from the UK is almost double the value of exports (see table **B**).

Kenya's trading partners

The EU, including the UK, is Kenya's main trading partner, accounting for over 50% of its trade. However, trade with Kenya's African

Exports to...	Value	Imports from...	Value
COMSA	45 000	European Union	63 480
European Union	39 060	UK	22 680
Uganda	19 060	UAE	13 860
Tanzania	15 160	South Africa	12 780
UK	12 340	Japan	12 500
Germany	8 820	Germany	10 240
Netherlands	6 380	India	9 620
Egypt	4 300	USA	8 800
USA	3 180	Saudi Arabia	8 460
South Africa	2 380	France	8 260

B Kenya's top ten importing/exporting partners, 1997 (KSh million)

neighbours is becoming more important. Kenya has a trade surplus with its immediate neighbours, Tanzania and Uganda. In 1999 these countries provided only 8.2% of Kenya's imports, but took 29.0% of its exports. Hydro-electric power comes from Uganda and vegetable oils from Tanzania. Kenya's largest export to its neighbouring countries is oil, which is imported from the Middle East and refined in Mombasa. Uganda is **landlocked** and uses Mombasa as its main coastal port (see figure **C**).

Kenya has formed trading unions with some of its African neighbours. These unions are similar to the European Union: they encourage trade between members. Kenya is also a member of COMSA, the Common Market for Eastern and Southern Africa, and EAC, the East African Cupertino trading union. Advantages of trading unions include:

- members can lift import taxes and controls on trade between them;
- there is a larger and more secure market – the EAC provides a market of 80 million people.

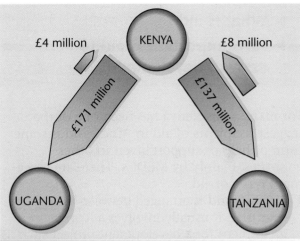

C Trade between Kenya, Uganda and Tanzania, 1999

Imports	1992	1994	1996		Exports	1992	1994	1996
Machinery	10 120	16 240	26 460		Tea	9500	16 880	22 700
Motor vehicles	2900	9520	15 800		Coffee	4120	13 060	16 420
Crude petroleum	10 980	14 400	13 500		Horticultural products	4180	8300	13 640
Iron & steel	3660	6220	9640		Petroleum products	4720	5060	7020
Plastics	2180	4260	7280		Cement	480	1640	2540
Wheat	680	2520	6380		Pyrethrum	740	1560	1600
Fertilizers	1500	3420	4820		Soda ash	540	980	1160
Paper products	960	1600	4100		Sisal	340	660	820

D Kenya's imports and exports, 1992–96 (KSh million)

	1990	1991	1992	1993	1994	1995	1996
Exports	24 880	31 040	34 840	72 500	83 420	93 120	119 380
Imports	50 920	52 920	59 100	101 120	115 080	115 160	168 480

E Total import and export values, 1990–96 (KSh million)

FACT FILE

Message from the Presidents

'We, the Presidents of Kenya, Tanzania and Uganda, have resolved to deepen and broaden the economic co-operation between the three countries for the short-, medium- and long-term benefit of the people. We have therefore created the Commission of East African Co-operation – whereby we can strive for the development of a single market and eventual economic integration. With the geographical ties and our own common history and culture, it is our conviction that in time, the East African region will become one of the most important trading blocks in the entire continent. We therefore invite international investors to share in the development of our region and also call on the donor community to support our endeavours.'
Daniel Arap Moi, Benjamin Mkapa, Yoweri Museveni
(*Financial Times Survey*, 5 November 1999.)

International aid

▶ **What is aid?**

▶ **How important is aid to Kenya's development?**

Main Donors	1991	1992	1993	1994	1995
Japan	198	129	142	129	199
Germany	55	68	55	46	42
Netherlands	26	54	48	42	36
USA	63	56	38	29	36
UK	66	47	39	44	35
Total aid received	**612**	**516**	**423**	**395**	**460**

A Main sources of bilateral aid to Kenya, 1991–95 (US$ million)

For many years Kenya has been one of the biggest recipients of aid in Africa. Aid is some form of help or support given to other countries, mainly by MEDCs. There are three main types of aid :

- **Bilateral aid** is arranged between two countries. It usually involves a loan or investment for a development project such as a new road, a power station or an industrial project that will help develop the economy of the recipient country. An example is the KSh800 million loan to Kenya by Germany to develop the Olkaria North East geothermal power station. The largest bilateral aid donors to Kenya are Japan, Germany, UK, Netherlands, France and the USA.

- **Multilateral aid** is given by international agencies such as the United Nations, the European Union or the International Monetary Fund. Many MEDCs give a proportion of their GNP every year to the agencies, which then decide how it is to be distributed. The UN recommends that each country donates 0.7% of its GNP to this fund, but not all countries manage this amount.

- **Voluntary aid** is given by charities such as Oxfam and ActionAid, which collect donations and use the money to develop

Date	Project	Cost (£)
1984–89	Kiambere hydro-electric power scheme (River Tana)	12.3 million
1985–91	Rehabilitation of Land Rovers	4.4 million
1988–93	Kenyan Agricultural Research Centre	7 million
1988–91	Assistance to Kenyan Railways	10 million
1992–93	Strengthening Primary Education	3.3 million

Source: Overseas Development Administration

C Major aid projects in Kenya funded by Britain

small-scale projects to improve the quality of life for people in Kenya, or to provide emergency aid.

Kenya's dependence on aid

Kenya received US$642 million in aid in 1999, which made up 14.6% of its GNP. In 1997 Kenya owed US$6.2 billion in debts. Over 50% was debt from multilateral aid projects, 38% from

B Some aid agencies working in Kenya

bilateral projects and 10% from commercial loans. Loans given to Kenya are usually given on condition that the country agrees to certain reforms. In 1991 many countries suspended their loans to Kenya until it made political and economic reforms.

Aid from Britain

Since its independence from Britain in 1963, Kenya has received over US$900 million in development assistance. In 1990 alone, Britain gave US$66 million (£44 million) to Kenya – only India, Bangladesh and Pakistan received more. British aid has mainly gone to programmes supporting the economic and social development of the country (figures **C** and **D**). The UK channels much of its aid through **non-governmental organizations** (NGOs), e.g. Oxfam.

Not all aid goes into long-term development projects. During 1997 and 1998, Britain provided over US$12 million for emergency relief operations to save lives, especially among pastoralists in northern Kenya, following drought in 1996/97 and then severe flooding in 1997/98.

Bilateral aid
(thousand UK£)

1990–91	49 728
1991–92	37 987
1992–93	36 525

Key
- Technical co-operation
- Project aid
- Food aid
- Disaster relief
- Other

How aid was spent in 1992–93

D British aid to Kenya, 1990–93

Debt: Forgiveness or Cancellation
An LEDC's debts are written off.
This happened in Egypt when the American government cancelled its debts in gratitude for its support in the Gulf War. The British government has also considered cancelling the debts of all LEDCs as a 'Millennium gesture'.

Debt for Equity Swaps
Debt is sold at a discount to multinationals that are interested in developing a project in an LEDC. The profits of the investment go to pay the debt. When it is paid off, all the additional profits go to the multinational.

Debt for Nature Swaps
An environmental group buys a debt from a country in return for a commitment to preserve environments within that country.

Debt Rescheduling
An extended time is given to pay off the loan.

E Tackling debt in LEDCs

FACT FILE

Emergency Food Aid
Twenty thousand tonnes of relief food, donated by USAid for northern Kenya are due in Mombasa tomorrow. Washington-based USAid assistant deputy administrator, Mr Len Rogers, announced this news during a tour of the Turkana District when he witnessed the difficulties of distributing relief caused by bad roads.

World Vision Kenya is battling against perilous conditions to make food available to the people in the drought stricken areas of the north. In Turkana, the largest district in the country, there are 205 relief distribution centres from which food is released to 331 000 affected people.

The team was shocked to see a shallow well where women and livestock compete for scarce, dirty brown water they scoop from sand. Whilst organizations such as World Food Programme and World Vision are addressing the need for emergency food supplies, the need for an adequate supply of clean water is also urgent. The District Water Officer informed the team that out of the 600 boreholes and shallow wells in Turkana, only 300 were functional. Some local residents travelled 50–60km in search of water. The District Officer has appealed to donors to consider long-lasting solutions such as the irrigation scheme in the Morulem area.
(Adapted from *Sunday Nation* – Nairobi, 9 July 2000.)

Aid for improving Kenya's roads

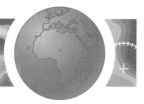

▶ **Why are road improvements needed?**

▶ **How will they be funded?**

Kenya's inadequate road network is under pressure from an increasing population, a growing economy and more and heavier vehicles. Kenya has 63 800km of roads, with only 8900 (14%) covered with tarmac. The extreme dry and rainy seasons often make unmade road surfaces impassable. In 1995, 2000 people were killed in traffic accidents in Kenya, partly due to a growing number of users with bad driving habits, but the need for road improvements is a priority. A good transport system is important for the country's economic development because:

- raw materials and manufactured goods need to be moved quickly;
- transport provides jobs;

The condition of the highways is something everyone seems to be complaining about. A ride on a *matatu* (minibus) is one of the cheapest ways of getting from A to B outside Nairobi. It is usually bumpier and longer than it need be because of the perilous state of some routes. Even outside the wet season, a trip to Lake Naivasha from the capital can be more like a rough ocean crossing, as the *matatu* navigates and sometimes sinks into the potholes in the red earth.

From the *Courier*

A Travelling in Kenya

B Road conditions in Kenya can be uncomfortable

- US$115 million will be allocated to repairing damaged roads in 26 urban centres.
- US$50 million will be used to repair the route linking Mombasa and Nairobi.
- The Kenyan government has agreed to maintain the road system, with 50% of the costs paid from its own budget.
- The government has agreed to attract private-sector money for maintenance and new road construction.
- The EU is funding improvements to sections of the roads between Sultan Hamund and Mtito Andei, and a section of the road between Mai-Mahiu and Naivasha.

- The EU has allocated funds to stop the deterioration of the Northern Corridor road to the west of Nairobi.
- Money has been allocated for emergency repairs to the Mombasa–Nairobi road.

Previous aid from the EU has paid for:

- improvements to the 103km link between Nairobi and the Uganda border, part of the Northern Corridor Transport Link;
- resurfacing the 51km trunk road between Kericho and Sotik in the main tea-growing area.

C Plans to improve the roads

- sometimes transport is the only effective form of communication between places, particularly in rural areas;
- tourism depends on quick and efficient transport.

The increases in traffic volume are due to several factors:

- There has been a sharp increase in the number of cars since the government reduced taxes on vehicles. There is a growing demand for luxury vehicles.
- The Nairobi–Naivasha road has seen a three-fold increase in the number of heavy lorries carrying freshly cut flowers for Kenya's rapidly expanding horticulture industry (see pages 36–37).
- The expanding tourist industry is putting more pressure on the roads as tourists seeking the 'safari experience' travel into the more remote areas.
- As Kenya expands its trade with its East African neighbours (Uganda and Tanzania), further pressure will be put on the roads leading to Mombasa, the biggest seaport in the region.

Multilateral aid supporting road improvements

There are two main sources of aid to help improve Kenya's road network:

- In 1995 the Kenyan government and the EU signed an agreement to redirect funds originally set aside for farming, into road improvements.
- In 1996 the World Bank agreed to give Kenya a loan of US$165 million to upgrade and maintain its roads. The loan will be repaid over 40 years.

Bilateral aid

Italy's support for road improvements in Kenya goes back to the 1940s. Italian prisoners-of-war were used to build the old road to Naivasha. On a bend in the road a chapel built by the prisoners and recently restored by the Kenyans bears testimony to their work. The Rironi–Mai section of the old Naivasha road has recently been rebuilt with $6.9 million of Italian aid.

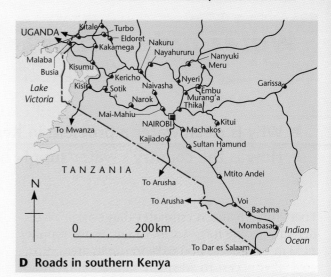

D Roads in southern Kenya

1992	1993	1994	1995	1996
Railways: goods traffic (thousand metric tonnes)				
2821	2310	1901	2090	1827
Roads: new motor vehicle registrations				
14 784	12 420	17 928	22 224	28 664

Source: Kenyan Ministry of Planning and Economic Development

E Rail and road transport in Kenya

FACT FILE

Expanding Kenya's air network
Eldoret International Airport is Kenya's newest and third international airport. Kenya's other international airports are the Jomo Kenyatta Airport in Nairobi and Moi Airport in Mombasa. This latest addition reflects the growing demand for international air transport fuelled by the growing tourist and horticulture trades. Located about 300km north-west of Nairobi, the airport can handle aircraft up to the size of a Boeing 767 or Airbus 310 and has adequate open space around it ready for commercial development.

Eldoret International Airport is situated in a rich agricultural area that is expected to feed it with cut flowers, fresh fruits and vegetables for export. The proximity of Eldoret town, just 6km away, is also a big advantage to the airport. The airport can be developed into a hub to serve the entire East African Region servicing the increasing trade links with Kenya's neighbours. Eldoret town is linked by road and rail to the tourist attractions of western Kenya and Uganda. Both the airport and the town have immense business opportunities waiting to be tapped.

Water aid

▶ **Why is clean water a problem in Kenya?**
▶ **How is the country's water supply being improved?**

The United Nations estimates that only 27% of Kenyan people have access to safe water supplies: 21% in rural areas and 61% in urban areas. Just 46% have access to adequate sanitation facilities. Kenya suffers from **water scarcity**.

Access to a supply of clean water is a problem in any country with unreliable, seasonal rainfall and poor storage facilities. Most Kenyans do not have water piped into their houses, so it has to be carried from a supply outside their homes – a river, lake, a well or a pump. It is usually the women and children who carry the water (photo **A**).

Many streams and rivers have become polluted in recent years as the population and industrial developments have increased. In rural areas where farming has become more intensive and more chemicals are being used, pollution is a growing problem. Poor planning and poor control of economic developments can have a negative effect on people and environments: 80% of all illnesses in the world are related to drinking contaminated water. Development projects to improve access to safe water often bring an improved quality of life for many people.

A Collecting water at Karungu, Lake Victoria

	Kenya	UK
1955	7189	51 199
1990	636	2090
2025*	235	1992

* UN estimate

B Availability of water in Kenya and the UK (millions of litres)

Tube wells

The best source of water for many people is a tube well. This is constructed by drilling a hole into the ground to tap an underground water supply (photo **C**). A simple hand-operated pump brings water to the surface. This is a good source of water because groundwater supplies are not usually polluted.

The Kenya Water for Health Organization (KWAHO) was started with the aim of involving people in providing and controlling their own water supply. This organization is a partnership with other groups. Village committees have been set up to involve the people in decisions about what type of water supply they need and how they are going to manage and maintain it. KWAHO encourages villagers to consider carefully the type of pump they need.

C A well in East Kitui

It must be:
- strong enough to stand up to a lot of work without breaking down;
- easy to repair and not needing expensive spare parts;
- easy for everyone to use, including children;
- able to pump water fast enough for people to fill their buckets before they get tired;
- made in Kenya, since there is not enough money to buy pumps from other countries;
- cheap to produce and repair.

Using rainwater

Tube wells are not suitable in all parts of Kenya. Sometimes the water is too deep underground for it to be pumped up by hand. One alternative is to save rainwater. Kenya has two seasons of heavy rainfall, but most of this water runs away unused. KWAHO helps schools to install 'rainwater harvesting' systems. Gutters are fitted to the roofs of schools, and downpipes then feed the water into tanks. Each tank can hold 80 000 litres. Children are appointed as water

D Rainwater harvesting system – collection tank being topped up

monitors to watch that the water is not wasted.

KWAHO is also helping schools to build cheap, hygienic latrines called the 'ventilated improved pit latrine', or VIP. Children dig a long deep trench, then a roof and cubicles are built over it.

FACT FILE

Low-cost solutions to water pollution

An unreliable supply of safe drinking water is one of Kenya's main barriers to development, particularly in the drought stricken northern regions. As the number of people living in rural areas increases, then increasing supplies of groundwater are being tapped. According to the World Wide Fund for Nature and the Lake Nakuru Conservation Development Project, most of the water which falls during the rainy season goes to waste because there is no effective way of harvesting it. Often the groundwater drawn through tube wells contains large amounts of dissolved heavy metals and impurities harmful to health. As agriculture becomes more intensive, an increasing number of pesticides find their way into groundwater and river supplies.

The World Wide Fund for Nature and the Lake Nakuru Conservation Development Project have developed a simple water purifier capable of filtering pesticide residue (organochlorine) and heavy metals. The water filter can remove about 50% of fluoride and 99% of pesticides and heavy metals contained in river water.

Nakuru District has one of the highest fluoride levels in water, most of which is extracted from boreholes. Fluoride causes the browning of teeth and makes bones brittle. Samples of water from River Ngosur, a permanent river that rises in Bahati and drains into Lake Nakuru, were found to contain pesticide residue, including the banned DDT. When the samples were filtered using filter candles, the entire pesticide residue was removed. The filter candles, which are made of ceramic materials, are available in local shops.

The filters are useful to people in the intensively farmed areas where sometimes more than 40 different types of pesticides are used. Some of the chemicals are washed into rivers by floodwater during the rainy season. The filters can also be used to clean run-off water in areas where farmers have dug water pans to harvest rainwater.
(Adapted from the *Daily Nation*, 6 July 2000.)

Health care

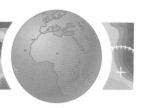

▶ **What health care problems does Kenya have?**

▶ **How is health care improving?**

Kenya's rapid economic development in recent years has had a major effect on many Kenyans' quality of life. Life expectancy increased from 45 years in 1960 to 57 years in 1998. This is a sign of better health conditions, yet health care provision for most Kenyan people is still inadequate (table **A**).

"The growing burden of ill health in Kenya (maternal mortality, malaria, HIV/AIDS and childhood illnesses) undermines people's chances of escaping from poverty."
DFID Country Strategy Report, 1999

Many of the illnesses and diseases that people suffer in Kenya are related to its geography as well as its development. Kenya is located in an area with a tropical climate and an unreliable supply of clean drinking water. So the major killer is malaria, followed by diseases linked with contaminated water supplies (table **B**). AIDS-related deaths are a recent and growing problem. By 1998, Kenya had 263 000 AIDS sufferers, and an estimated 800 000 more people were HIV carriers.

The Kenyan government and aid agencies have channelled a lot of money into building new hospitals. Most of these are concentrated in urban centres (map **C**). Nairobi has three times the national average of hospital beds, but people in rural areas are not so well provided for. Most Kenyans live in rural areas and transport to hospital is often impossible.

	Kenya	UK
% of people with access to health services	77	100
(in rural areas of Kenya)	(40)	
Infant mortality (per 1000)	51	7
% of children born underweight	16	7
Daily calorie supply as % of requirements	89	130
% of births attended by a doctor or nurse	28	100

A Health figures: a comparison between Kenya and the UK

Illness/disease	No. of cases reported	% of total illness
Diarrhoea	823 096	4.7
Malaria	4 099 138	23.3
Intestinal worms	788 455	4.5
Eye infections	449 123	2.5
Respiratory diseases	3 418 119	19.5
Ulcers and skin disorders	1 289 180	7.3
Rheumatics and joint disorders	473 275	2.7
Accidents	399 742	2.3

B The most common diseases

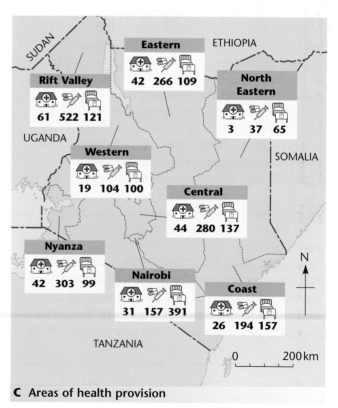

Key

🏥 Number of hospitals

💉 Number of health centres and dispensaries

🛏 Beds per 100 000 people

C Areas of health provision

Preventative care

'Prevention is better than cure' is the motto of the World Health Organization (WHO). WHO, the British Government Department for International Development, and many charities, all support the Kenyan government in small-scale preventative medicine projects, particularly in rural areas. These programmes include:

- a widespread campaign to inoculate against major diseases – by 1998, 73% of Kenya's infant population had been immunized;
- local family planning centres, which provide advice on sexually transmitted diseases to try and stop the spread of HIV/AIDS;
- setting up small-scale health centres and dispensaries in rural areas – these supply basic medicines which may be bought locally in village stores;
- extending the supply of clean drinking water.

COMMUNITY-BASED HEALTH CARE IN MPEKETONI

Mpeketoni is a settlement on the coast of Kenya about 50km from Lamu. The settlement was started in 1972 as part of a resettlement scheme for landless people. It was a chance for people to own land for the first time. But the swampy ground on the edge of a lake was infested with mosquitoes. A poor supply of fresh water and no proper latrines added to the health problems.

In 1984 Oxfam started a community-based health programme in Mpeketoni. The programme helps people care for their own health in their own community. Community health workers (CHW) are chosen by the community and live and work in the villages. The CHW are medically trained by Oxfam and are in charge of the programme themselves.

Each CHW is responsible for 20 farms and travels around the farms on a bike provided by Oxfam for the community.

This programme has brought real improvements in local health care.

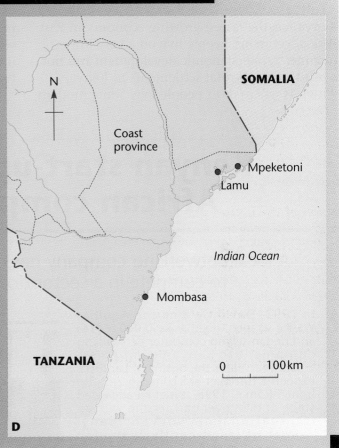

D

FACT FILE

New government health policy planned

The Medical Services Minister of the Kenyan Government, Amukowa Anangwe, announced a new five-year national health plan at a medical exhibition held in Nairobi in July 2000. The plan is aimed at making health care delivery more efficient and cost-effective. The Minister called for more research and development into treatments for diseases afflicting the poor, such as tuberculosis, sleeping sickness, AIDS and malaria.

Malaria accounts for 3% of illnesses in the world, yet only 0.1% of global research funds are spent on its cure. Several drug manufacturing companies have reduced the price of anti-retroviral medicines for AIDS sufferers, but the drugs are still inaccessible to the poorest.

IT and two kinds of development

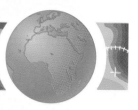

▶ **What new IT developments have been introduced in Kenya?**

IT has two meanings for economic development in Kenya. IT means Information Technology at one end of the development scale, but it also means Intermediate Technology at the other end.

Kenya has the fastest-growing economy in East Africa, yet many people live on a very low income. Rapid economic development has not spread to many rural settlements in Kenya, which is where most people live. Some modern advances, for example internet access, which come with rapid economic growth, are only found in Kenya's cities and wealthier regions. They would be totally out of place in villages without electricity and with only basic **amenities**. Appropriate or intermediate technology, providing sustainable fuel or clean water supplies, would improve the quality of life for local people. Extracts **A** and **B** describe two IT success stories in Kenya.

Kenyan start-up succeeds in African computer niche

A local networking company has overcome funding obstacles to compete in a sector dominated by the West

In 1993, David Gatama and Aquinas Wasike scraped together Ks50,000 (£416) and began selling computer networking equipment to Kenyan companies.

Six years later the business, Lantech, expects a turnover of $10m (£6.2m), up from $4.5m in 1998. It is at an advanced stage of talks over partnership with an international network company.

With offices recently opened in Tanzania and Uganda, Lantech claims it is now East Africa's leader in providing equipment that connects computers in a network. "With our international partnership, we are looking to triple our growth rate," says Musili Nzambu, managing director.

It is an impressive tale for a home-grown company in a country where economic growth has fallen for three years, and where information technology is dominated by Western multinationals. Lantech's employees are all Kenyans.

Financial Times, 12 August 1999

A Information technology

Success Story: Upesi Stoves in Kenya

The British charity Intermediate Technology has been working in Kenya to set up the IT Stoves and Household Energy programme (SHE). This project has focused on very poor rural households and works with local women's groups who make the stoves. One type of improved stove, the Upesi, has been very successful.

The word *upesi* means 'fast' in Swahili. It is a well-chosen name for the pottery cylinder which is built into a mud surround in kitchens. It burns fuel more efficiently and speeds up the whole cooking process.

The Upesi is designed to burn wood or biomass fuels such as crop waste or maize stalks. The Upesi burns more efficiently, so it needs less fuel and women have to spend less time collecting it.

The stove also produces less smoke, and because women spend less time cooking, they are less exposed to smoke. Tests have shown that in homes where Upesi stoves are used, the number of children suffering from respiratory diseases and conjunctivitis has reduced by 60–70%.

As well as benefits for the users, women's groups who produce and sell the stoves have a sustainable income. Several thousands of the stoves are made each year. Women who used to earn Ks50–100 (about £1) a day selling vegetables at a market can now earn Ks150–200 selling the stoves.

Now a new portable stove has been designed to give poor people in rural areas more choice.

B Intermediate technology

FACT FILE

Information, communication and media

Kenyan people are beginning to appreciate the benefits of the modern communication revolution. There is a growing number of Kenyan companies set up to access the information superhighway. These are allowing Kenyan industries to access a wider range of customers and have a more competitive edge in today's global market.

The Kenyan public is also beginning to benefit from access to a range of television and radio stations. Since the government partially liberalized the airwaves about two years ago, shifting from state control of the media, more than 20 radio stations and 12 TV stations have been licensed.

Although there are a growing number of remote smaller towns and villages becoming connected to national stations, most of the growth is focused in the larger towns and cities.

Two new radio stations have just gone on air. Kiss FM started broadcasting in Nairobi in July 2000. The managing director of the station said 'We shall focus on music, entertainment, fun, local and international news targeted at urban professionals between 20 and 35.' Iqra Broadcast Network, owned by the Supreme Council of Kenyan Muslims, has also begun broadcasting specifically for Kenya's Muslim community.

Women in Kenya

▶ How is the role of women changing in Kenya?

Women Making Political Waves

Meandeleo ya Wanawake (Progress through Women)

National Council of Women in Kenya

Kenya Women Finance Trust

The Green Belt Movement – women to replant trees

A Some newspaper headlines

Since Independence in 1963, Kenyan women have become far more active in their country's development, for example through politics, and in environmental and economic projects (figure A).

In spite of the growth in Kenya's urban areas (see page 22), most Kenyans still live in rural areas. In fact more men than women have moved into urban areas, leaving a higher percentage of women in the countryside. Today, 30% of families in Kenya are single-parent families, leaving women as the main bread-winners and home-makers.

Many problems face women who want to improve their standard of living.
- Most land is owned by men – when a father dies the land is divided between his sons.
- Women find it very difficult to borrow money to develop a business.
- Far fewer girls than boys receive adequate education.
- Many Kenyans still work their own land, but many others are moving into direct employment where they are paid a wage. In 1990 only about 20% of Kenyans in paid employment were women, and these were usually in low-skilled, low-paid jobs.

The changing role
But things are changing for Kenyan women. Many women in rural areas are setting up small businesses. Others have been involved in the introduction of labour-saving technology, which has given them more time to develop other interests. Women have also become much more involved with politics. In Nairobi there is an Education Centre for Women in Democracy. One of the Centre's main aims is to **empower** women to stand as candidates in legislative elections.

Grace Githi, the head of a busy law practice in Nairobi, set up the Institute for Education in Democracy, which aims to promote democracy through education.

Women in rural areas
The Manyoya women's group was started in 1985 as part of the Shambere rural education programme in western Kenya. The project aimed

B Wangari Maathai, founder of the Green Belt Movement, winning the Edinburgh Medal in 1993. Her organization has involved 50 000 women, planting 20 million trees, since 1977.

to solve the problems of large numbers of unemployed school-leavers by providing training in skills that people could use to earn a living.

The Manyoya group were trained to spin wool and knit jumpers. Garments made by the group were exhibited at national craft fairs, and as a result two shops in Nairobi contracted the group to provide the shops with sweaters. The demand was so high that they were unable to produce them quickly enough, and more women were employed. The initial training was provided by a volunteer from Britain. Later the group were given training in marketing the products. They soon established themselves as a trade association controlling their own finances and bank account. The Manyoya sweaters are now sold in high-class shops to tourists.

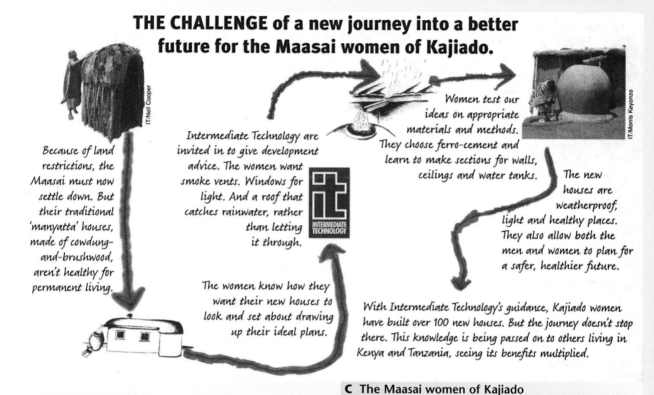

THE CHALLENGE of a new journey into a better future for the Maasai women of Kajiado.

Because of land restrictions, the Maasai must now settle down. But their traditional 'manyatta' houses, made of cowdung-and-brushwood, aren't healthy for permanent living.

Intermediate Technology are invited in to give development advice. The women want smoke vents. Windows for light. And a roof that catches rainwater, rather than letting it through.

Women test our ideas on appropriate materials and methods. They choose ferro-cement and learn to make sections for walls, ceilings and water tanks.

The new houses are weatherproof, light and healthy places. They also allow both the men and women to plan for a safer, healthier future.

The women know how they want their new houses to look and set about drawing up their ideal plans.

With Intermediate Technology's guidance, Kajiado women have built over 100 new houses. But the journey doesn't stop there. This knowledge is being passed on to others living in Kenya and Tanzania, seeing its benefits multiplied.

C The Maasai women of Kajiado

FACT FILE

'Harambee'

'Harambee' or self-help, is a concept formally introduced by Kenya's first leader, President Kenyatta. This has been continued under president Moi. Self-help projects raise funds or get a community working together on specific projects to improve the quality of life for local people. Kenyan women's groups have used the harambee tradition to improve agriculture, education, health care, rural water supplies and forestry. There is a long history of women assisting one another on a collective basis in Kenya.

In the 1950s women's groups were formalized and became registered with the government, In 1976 the government set up a Women's Bureau within the Ministry of Culture and Social Services. Rapid growth in numbers followed: there were 4300 groups registered at the late 1970s, 16 000 by the late 1980s, and now there are over 27 000.

Women's groups are particularly useful to women in rural areas, from low-income households and often single parents. They can provide:

• opportunities to generate income, such as selling handicrafts and farm produce;
• access to extra labour at critical times, such as harvest times;
• ways to save and invest to improve their quality of life;
• support for child care or attending sick family members;
• ways for the community to raise money for community projects such as health centres, schools and water-harvesting projects.

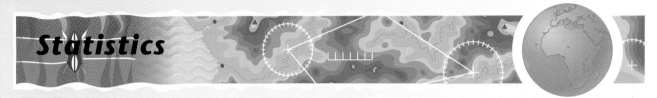

Statistics

	UK	KENYA	BRAZIL	FRANCE	USA
Total area (km²)					
Total population (millions)					
Population density: people per km²					

Population

	UK	KENYA	BRAZIL	FRANCE	USA
Birth rate (per 1 000) people					
Death rate (per 1 000) people					
Life expectancy (male and female)	74M 79F	54M 55F	57M 66F	75M 83F	73M 79F
Fertility (children per female)	2	6	3	2	2
Population structure: 0–14 15–59 60+	19% 61% 21%	50% 46% 4%	35% 58% 7%	20% 61% 19%	21% 62% 17%
Urban population (% of population)	90%	25%	78%	74%	77%

Environment and economy

	UK	KENYA	BRAZIL	FRANCE	USA
Rate of urban population change	−0.5%	1.2%	0.3%	0%	0.8%
Land use (%): arable grass forest	27 46 10	3 67 4	7% 22% 58%	33 20 27	19 25 30
% workforce in: farming industry services	2 28 70	81 7 12	25% 25% 50%	6 29 65	3 25 72
GNP per person (US$)	$18 700	$280	$3 640	$24 990	$26 980
Energy used (tonnes/person/year)	5.40	0.11	0.44	5.43	10.74

Society and quality of life

	UK	KENYA	BRAZIL	FRANCE	USA
Infant mortality (deaths per 1000 births)	6	55	53	6	7
People per doctor	300	10 000	1000	333	420
Food supply (calories per person per day)	3 317	2 075	2 824	3 633	3 732
Adult literacy	99%	75%	81%	99%	99%
TVs per 1000 people	448	18	220	589	805
Personal computers per 1000 people	186	1	13	134	328
Aid received or given per person	$53 given	$42 received	$2 given	$137 given	$33 given
Spending on education (as % of GNP)	5.3	6.8	3.7	6.0	7.0
Spending on military (as % of GNP)	4.0	2.8	1.2	3.4	5.3
United Nations Human Development Index (out of 1.0)	0.93	0.46	0.81	0.95	0.94

Figures are for 1993–98. Source: *Philip's Geographical Digest* (United Nations, World Bank). The Human Development Index is worked out by the UN. It is a summary of national income, life expectancy, adult literacy and education. It is a measure of human progress. In 1998, the HDI ranged from 0.19 to 0.96 (Canada).

General

Longest river: Tana
Highest point: Mt. Kenya (5 199m)
Lowest point: Indian Ocean (0m)
Largest City and Capital: Nairobi (2 100 000)
Languages: English, Swahili and numerous
   indigenous languages

Ethnic groups: Kikuyu – 22%, Luhya – 14%, Luo – 13%, Kalenjin – 12%, Kamba – 11%, Kisii – 6%. Meru – 6%, other African – 15%, non African (European, Asian and Arab – 1%).
Religion: Protestant – 38%, Roman Catholic – 28%, indigenous beliefs – 26%, Muslim – 7%, other – 1%
Currency: 1 Kenyan Shilling – 100 cents (about 80p (*The World Fact Book, Kenya*)

Communications

Telephones	290 000
Mobile phones	6 000
Radios	3 070 000
Televisions	730 000

Railways	2 778 km
Highways	63 800 kms (paved 8 868, unpaved 54 932)
Airports	230 (paved 21, unpaved 209)
Ports	Kisumu, Lamu, Mombasa

Land Area Statistics

Land area	580 379 km^2
Water	13 400 km^2
Land Boundaries	3 446 km

Borders

Ethiopia	830 km
Somalia	682 km
Sudan	232 km
Tanzania	769 km
Uganda	933 km
Coastline	536 km

Largest settlements

Nairobi	2 100 000
Mombasa	465 0000
Kisumu	185 100
Nakuru	162 800
Eldoret	104 900
Nyeri	88 600
Mere	78 100
Thika	57 100
Kitale	53 000
Kisii	44 000
Kericho	40 000

Main Exports Value (KSh)

Tea	22 700
Coffee	16 420
Horticultural Products	13 420
Petroleum Products	7 020

Main Imports Value (KSh)

Machinery	26 460
Motor Vehicles	15 800
Crude Petroleum	13 500
Iron and Steel	9 640

Electricity Facts

Production	4 078 billion kWh
Method of production:	
Fossil fuel	8.27%
Hydro	82.74%
Nuclear	0%
Other	8.99%

Main Trading Partners (1996)

Exports		Imports	
Uganda	16.1%	UK	12%
Tanzania	12.8%	UAE	9%
UK	10.4%	US	8%
		Japan	8%

Glossary

agro-industry commercial farming carried out on a large scale, typically by transnational companies

altitude height of the land – it has an important influence on climate, vegetation and agriculture

amenities purpose-built facilities

arid dry

birth rate the number of births in a year per 1000 of the total population

cash crop growing a crop or rearing animals to sell for profit

colony a country that has been taken under the political and economic control of another country. Most 'colonies' were developing countries; the colonial powers were developed countries

commercial farm farm that produces goods to sell – the aim is to make a profit

comparative advantage the advantage some countries or regions have to produce goods better or more cheaply than less favoured regions

contraception any form of birth control

cosmopolitan consisting of people from many parts of the world

crustal plate the sections of crust that make up the Earth's outer layer

death rate the number of deaths in a year per 1000 of the total population

deforestation removal of trees (and other vegetation) for farming, fuelwood and timber resources

desertification the spread of desert conditions into non-desert areas

ecosystem a set of links between vegetation, climate, and other parts of the environment

ecotourism travelling to areas to appreciate the natural environment, and bringing income to the area without causing permanent damage

empower to give power to people to enable them to make independent decisions and choices

escarpment a continuous line of steep slopes, facing in the same direction and caused by erosion of folded rock

extensive subsistence farming subsistence farming using a large amount of land in a way that produces a low yield per hectare

extinct volcano a volcano which has not erupted since records began, and is unlikely to erupt again

fault lines of weakness or fractures in the Earth's crust where earthquakes have occurred, displacing rock on one or both sides

fertility rate the number of children born to each woman

formal employment employment registered with the government for tax purposes

GNP (Gross National Product) a measure of the wealth created by a country's business both at home and abroad

GNP per head the average amount of wealth each person within a country has

higher-order services shops and services which people buy less often, and travel further to buy, e.g. furniture or electrical goods

hinterland the area around a settlement which serves, and is served by it

horticultural produce intensive production of flowers, fruit and vegetables

humidity the amount of water vapour in the atmosphere

humus rotting vegetation in a soil

import substitution where a country produces its own goods to avoid costly imports

indigenous the first people to settle an area

informal employment employment not registered with the government for tax e.g. street vending

informal settlement areas where people, often new migrants in an urban area, have built homes on land without permission

in-migration the movement of people into an area on a permanent or semi-permanent basis

intensive farming getting maximum output by using high inputs of machinery, irrigation and other technologies

labour intensive needing large inputs of human labour – rather than machinery – to perform a task

landlocked a country with no access to the sea

lapse rate the rate at which air changes temperature with a change in height

liberalize to free from restrictions and regulations

life expectancy how long a person can expect to live

literacy the ability to read and write

malaria fever caused by a parasite, transmitted by the bite of a female malarial mosquito

mangrove swamp areas of low trees and shrubs which grow on mudflats in tropical coastal areas

marginal land land that is difficult to cultivate and which yields little profit

migrate to move from place to place

molten magma material found below the Earth's crust

monsoon sudden wet season within the tropics

multinational a company or corporation that operates in several countries

natural increase the increase in population caused by the difference between the birth rate and the death rate

newly industrializing country an LEDC that has industrialized over the past 20 years and has had a high rate of economic growth

nomadic pastoralist a person who moves with their animals in search of water and pasture

non-governmental organization an organization not belonging to or associated with a government

out-migration the movement of people out of an area

pastoral farmers farmers who breed and rear animals

plantation large estates on which crops such as tea or coffee are grown for sale

primary product a product of farming, fishing, forestry and mining industries

pyrethrum a flower which contains a chemical used as insecticide

resource capacity the amount of resources available for use

sanitation hygienic disposal of waste products

savanna tropical grassland, often with scattered trees

semi-arid areas that receive about 350–500 mm of rain each year with seasonal drought

settlement any form of human habitation, from a single house to the largest city

shamba small farmholding in Kenya

soil erosion the removal of soil by water and wind at a rate greater than soil is being created

staple food main basic food source for people, mainly in developing countries, e.g. maize

subsistence farming farmers grow food for their own needs and not to sell

sustainable the use of resources and technology that do not harm the natural environment or affect the long-term supply of resources

terraces steps cut into hillsides to make flat areas of land for farming and to control erosion

trade balance the balance between the income received from exports and the amount paid for imports

trade deficit the shortfall of exports compared with imports

trade winds tropical easterly winds blowing towards the Equator from the north-east and south-east from sub-tropical anticyclones

tree line the line beyond which trees will not grow, at high altitudes or at high latitudes

urbanization the increase and growth of towns and urban areas

water scarcity short of water for basic needs

World Trade Organization organization of the main trading nations in the world which advise on the regulation of trade

Finding out more about Kenya

http://www.kenyaweb.com

http://www.africaonline.co.uk

http://www.rcbowen.com/kenya

http://www.hsk.org.uk

http://www.kenyabirds.org.uk

http://www.kenyaflowers.co.uk

http://www.kenya-wildlife-service.org

http://www.meteo.go.ke

http://www.nationaudio.com/news/dailynation/today

http://www.peopleandplanet.net

Index

Bold type refers to terms included in the glossary.
Italic type refers to photographs or maps